METAL ENAMELING

Cast silver pendant. Ruth Tepping.

Color II. Mural on several levels. Pauli Lame.

METAL ENAMELING

by POLLY ROTHENBERG

CROWN PUBLISHERS, INC., NEW YORK

*To creative craftsmen everywhere who find pleasure
in sharing their experiences with others*

Fourth Printing, August,1974

Library of Congress Catalog Card Number: 70–75079

Printed in the United States of America
Published simultaneously in Canada by
General Publishing Company Limited

Designed by Shari de Miskey

Acknowledgments

It is with sincere appreciation that I acknowledge the contribution of the dedicated, talented, and friendly artists whose inspired works are pictured in this book. Many of them took valuable time to acquire new photographs of their work for inclusion in this volume. I want to thank the staff of *Ceramics Monthly Magazine* who have graciously allowed me to include in the book pictures and material of mine that have appeared in their publication. Thanks to the Research and Education Department of the American Craftsmen's Council and to *Craft Horizons* for favors and permission to use certain pictures that have been published in their magazine. Thanks, also, to Dr. Warren Kreye and his wife, Audrea, for allowing me access to their notes and equipment for the electroforming of copper. Finally, my special thanks go to my husband, Maurice, for his understanding and sympathetic cooperation.   P.R.

*Projects and photographs by
Polly Rothenberg, unless
otherwise indicated.*

Contributing Artists

AARIS, HAMILTON P., OREGON
BRADY, JUSTIN, INDIANA
COFFMAN, BARBARA, WISCONSIN
CONNER, MAE, OHIO
DRERUP, KARL, NEW HAMPSHIRE
EISENBERG, MARGUERITE, OHIO
ELSBREE, MIRIAM, PENNSYLVANIA
ENGSTROM, AUDREY, MICHIGAN
ENGSTROM, ROBERT, MICHIGAN
ERIKSON, SIGURD ALF, OSLO, NORWAY
FISCH, ARLINE, CALIFORNIA
FRANKEL, CHARLES, CALIFORNIA
FRANKEL, DEXTRA, CALIFORNIA
GEBERT, LINDA, KANSAS
GEHL, WILLIAM, INDIANA
HASSELSCHWERT, HAROLD, OHIO
HELITZER, ELINOR, KANSAS
HULTBERG, PAUL, NEW YORK
KREYE, AUDREA, OHIO
KREYE, WARREN, OHIO
KRISTENSEN, GAIL, MINNESOTA
LAME, PAULI, ARIZONA
LOVING, RICHARD, ILLINOIS
MCDERMOTT, MARY ELLEN, OHIO
MAGDEN, NORMAN, OHIO
MARKUS, RUTH, OHIO
MASRIERA Y CARRERAS, BARCELONA, SPAIN
MERRICK, NOEL, INDIANA
MUNTER, CATHERINE, WASHINGTON
NICHOLS, GERRI, OHIO
REICHENBERGER, NELLA, PENNSYLVANIA
ROTHENBERG, POLLY, OHIO
RUNYON, TREVA, OHIO
SCHWARCZ, JUNE, CALIFORNIA
SHARP, MARY, CALIFORNIA
SKAGGS, LILLIAN, OREGON
SLAUGHTER, PATRICIA, INDIANA
STABLER, HAROLD, LONDON, ENGLAND
STABLER, PHOEBE, LONDON, ENGLAND
STRAUSS, CLAIRE L., NEW YORK
TEPPING, RUTH, OHIO
WEBB, RAMA, KANSAS

Contents

List of Color Illustrations

Foreword

The growing trend toward brilliant color in handcrafted functional and decorative art objects has increased the appreciation for well-designed enamels. The speed and ease with which these colorful pieces can be created have, in recent years, encouraged a surge of interest in this craft of fusing a smooth glassy coating to metals. The equipment is simple; not much space is required for the work. Major manufacturers make available a considerable variety of vibrant ready-ground enamel colors. In spite of the increasing interest and involvement in this art, good designs are sometimes left unfinished when a craftsman becomes disheartened by lack of knowledge about processes for developing his ideas. This book is designed to meet the problems encountered by the author during actual construction of pieces.

The work provides some techniques not generally found in books on enameling. For example, the section on footed bowls has detailed instructions and step-by-step illustrations for soldering in the kiln and for the enameling of soldered pieces. Specific directions on the use of art glass in enamel designs should assist craftsmen who have found this process to be a source of frustration. Instructions on setting up and using electroforming equipment are detailed in the section on experimental enameling. No methods are described that have not been tested.

Enameling methods and projects progress from the easiest to the most complicated, and include detailed step-by-step illustrations. Technical problems are discussed in their logical sequence. Throughout the book, language is employed that can be easily understood by student and craftsman alike. Commercial aids such as firescale remover, etching mordants, various pickling compounds, enameling gums, and tools that smooth the path for enamelists are suggested and demonstrated where they do not sacrifice handcrafting.

The projects are intended as guides for processes; they are not suggested as models to be copied. However, methods and suggestions are offered on ways of developing designs, based on the nature of the materials involved. Sometimes when a craftsman is learning a new skill, the strangeness of the materials and tools may temporarily thwart ideas for design. Experience in the handling of enamels should overcome this problem. Eventually, the alert enamel craftsman will feel at ease with the materials, tools, and processes, and he will begin to think of design as an integral part of construction.

Most enameling methods can be carried out with a few basic tools. The required equipment is discussed and illustrated. Although there are many well-designed basic shapes available, when an enamelist becomes familiar with the tools, materials, and proc-

esses, he may yearn to cut and form some of his own metal shapes. Steps in construction and required equipment for forming a basic shape and contoured sculptural pieces are described and fully illustrated. There is detailed description of enameling the hand-formed sculpture.

Because it is the author's belief that techniques in any field should first be conquered on a basic level, even the more complex processes are simplified and easy to follow. Throughout the pages there are photographs of the work of many skilled and talented craftsmen, illustrating the wide variety in creative expression when the art of enameling is developed to its high potential. The methods herein described may be modified; others may be added or substituted. They represent no arbitrary rules. Each craftsman will combine what he learns with his own experience to work out a comfortable system for his individual needs.

Divider. Dextra and Charles Frankel. Enameled copper repoussé and enameled copper on heliarced pieces with copper pipe frame, 8 feet high by 4 feet wide by 12 inches thick. For the residence of Mr. and Mrs. Lloyd Beck, Beverly Hills, California. Courtesy of the artists. *Photo by Richard Gross.*

Introduction

Metal enameling is an art so ancient, its beginnings are lost in obscurity. But until the present century, only the wealthy could buy or commission a fine enamel. Indeed, historically, it was customary for members of both nobility and the church to support and carefully nurture the talents of enamel craftsmen so they could spend all their time creating priceless enamels for their patrons alone. A tight society of craft guilds perpetuated the system.

In our time, anyone who loves beauty may buy or create enamels. They are not reserved for any privileged class. In this fluid society, occasional sporadic efforts to revive the guild system have been ineffectual. Traditionally, enamel richly adorned exquisite and finely crafted metalwork. Today, innovative breakthroughs in technology and attitude have brought bold and startling new colors and methods to metal enameling. Artist-craftsmen with talent and skill continue to make exquisite small and refined articles, but they are designed with the lively and fascinating freedom characteristic of contemporary art. Plique-à-jour and cloisonné have taken on an airy grace. Dynamic metal forms such as electro formed copper and cast silver wear their own enamel jewels. Ancient techniques appear in modern architecture. Exciting treatment brings an ever-increasing range of experimental approaches to traditional processes.

The emotional excitement combined with the disciplined approach required in working with intense heat, metal, and molten silicates makes metal enameling both a reward and a challenge. How thrilling it is to take a piece of clean metal, apply a layer of ground enamel over it, put it into a hot kiln for a few moments, and then carefully withdraw a glowing, colorful, and vibrant creation uniquely one's own!

1

Enameled bowl. June Schwarcz. Hammered copper bowl with electroformed copper lines fused into the bowl's white enameled exterior. Collection of Shirley Sagal. Courtesy of the artist. *Photo by Bob Harwayne.*

Silver tiara. Arline Fisch. Plique-à-jour in blue, gold, and green transparent enamels. Forged silver wire construction. Separate sections of ⅛-inch bezel wire for frames were soft-soldered into place when completed. Arline Fisch teaches at San Diego State College. Courtesy of the artist. *Photo by Lynn Fayman's Studio.*

AN APPROACH TO DESIGN IN ENAMELING

Every material has certain inherent qualities originating in or derived from its uniqueness. Clay has plasticity, and it is easily shaped, but when it is fired it becomes hard and rocklike. Wool, which is fibrous, can be combed, spun, and woven. Enamel, too, has special characteristics that should be taken into account by the sensitive craftsman who is seeking a base or starting point from which to develop his designs. Let us consider some of the qualities peculiar to enamel, and how they may be exploited.

Some Enamels Transmit Light

This is a quality possessed by neither clay nor wool. When *transparent* enamels are fired over hammered metal, light is refracted and is transmitted through them into brilliant and changing hues. Too much surface enrichment would cover and conceal this quality; but a blending of transparent colors would enhance its limpid depth.

Enamels Are Colorful

When transparents are fired over opaque enamels of similar hue, they emphasize and deepen the richness of the opaque colors. For example, when transparent turquoise is fired over prefired opaque turquoise or robin's-egg blue, it gives a startling depth and beauty. Enamels display their radiant colors to advantage when one subtle hue is laid over or against another, shading and melting into iridescence.

Enamels Are Glossy

They should not be dulled to resemble

Candy dish. Treva Runyon. The cloisonné design shows new, delicate use of cloisonné wire as a silvery line in a visual idea. Inlays of foil highlight parts of the cloisons. They are carved with transparent blue and green. Mrs. Runyon teaches art at Miami University, Oxford, Ohio. Courtesy of the artist.

pottery. They can be combined with or mounted against materials that are not glossy, such as oxidized metal, wood, and textured surfaces. In a softly lighted room, a gleaming bowl or tray in shades of one color will catch and reflect light, enhancing the entire area. These monochromatic glossy accent pieces are used extensively in contemporary interiors.

Some Enamel Colors Are Delicate; Some Are Intense

Sensitive tracery patterns may further emphasize subtle colors. Rich dark colors laid against delicate hues, such as purple against pink, provide pleasing contrast. Bold patterns exploit bright, bold opaques. Black accents may sharpen designs that seem too pastel.

Enamels Become Fluid at High Temperatures

Because enamel melts when it is fired, it tends to flow downward on steep-sided pieces. Opaque and transparent colors laid over and above one another will flow, merge, and combine to form intricate organic variations on a high-fired piece.

The development of designs incorporating these and other essential characteristics of enamel is determined by the individual craftsman's interpretations of these qualities. Color and design are personal, and involve the mind as well as the eye. The blue pattern one person sees may not be the same blue pattern as experienced by another person. Each craftsman will add something of his own imagery, which should take into account the unique qualities of the materials involved.

Engraved champlevé pendant. Harold Hasselschwert. Exquisitely designed pure silver enameled pendant displays the craftsman's superb skill as an engraver and enamelist. Tiny chased depressions are filled with transparent blues, greens, and brown enamel. Mr. Hasselschwert is Professor of Art, Bowling Green University, Ohio.

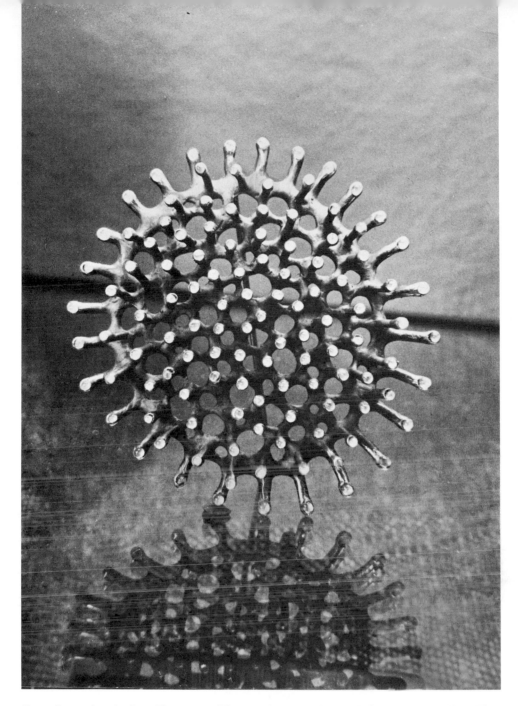

Cast silver pin. Audrey Engstrom. The sturdy metal has a delicate lacy quality. Tiny transparent enamel jewels tip each silver dendrite. Courtesy of the artist. *Photo by Robert Engstrom.*

Materials

ENAMELS

Enamel is composed of a basic frit and various metallic oxides for color and opacity. Like glass, enamels are silicates. They must have certain qualities to assist them in fusing to metals and to give them brilliance, elasticity, and stability. Potash, lime, and silica (sand) in specified proportions produce clear glass. Potash and soda contribute sparkle and elasticity. These ingredients are combined with oxide of lead and borax for degrees of hardness or softness. Borax also aids enamel in uniting with the metallic oxides that give enamels their vibrant colors. For example, oxide of copper produces turquoise and green. Iron oxides make some browns, greens, and blacks. Other ingredients are opacifiers for making opaques and opalescents.

The oxides are combined with the other ingredients, and melted together for several hours in a furnace. When mature, they are poured out to cool on steel slabs. The resultant sheets of enamel are broken into chunks, pulverized in large ball mills, then strained and sorted according to mesh size. Brilliance, stability, and color depend upon perfect intimacy of combination of component parts and maintainance of temperature throughout the fusion.

Several types of enamels are made commercially: transparent, opaque, and translucent 80-mesh ground dry enamels; 200- to 400-mesh opaques, either dry or suspended in a painting medium for brush application; lump enamel in transparent and opaque; hard granular enamels in 8- to 14-mesh, suitable for texture effects; opaque crackles; and other novelty enamels. Overglaze, black underglaze, and metallic lusters are useful for decorative effects, and they remain distinct when fired at recommended temperatures. In general, enamels are fired at temperatures from 1350° F. to 1600° F. Enamels fired at the lower temperatures are called *soft;* those fired higher are *hard* enamels.

Transparent Enamels

Light can pass through fired transparent enamels. These enamels depend for their beauty on light reflected through them from the metal underneath. They reveal their greatest brilliance and clarity when they are washed before they are used. Although they fuse at lower temperatures than opaque enamels, their true depth and greatest transparency develop when they are fired at higher temperatures, around 1500° F.

Opaque Enamels

Opaque colors cover and conceal the metals or enamels over which they are fired. When they are overfired, opaques tend to become translucent, but a subsequent firing at lower temperature, about 1400° F., will restore their opacity.

Translucent Enamels

If they are fired too hot, translucent enamels tend to become transparent. When

Perfume bottle. Audrey Engstrom. Pure silver, cast and soldered. Tops of both sections unscrew. Blue transparent enamel jewels. Courtesy of the artist. *Photo by Robert Engstrom.*

Champlevé cups. Mary Sharp. Copper with blue enamels. Courtesy of the artist.

properly matured, they have a delicate translucent quality comparable to an opal. Opalescent enamel colors display their full beauty when they are applied over a coat of fired, colorless, transparent flux enamel.

Liquid Flux

Liquid flux enamel can be poured, dipped, brushed, or trailed. It is especially useful for application to the inside of a narrow or tubular shape. It fires to a colorless transparent glassy coat. It should be fired near 1500° F. for true transparency.

Crackles

Crackle enamel is available in liquid or dry form. These enamels are intended for decorative use over a base coat of fired enamel, for a crackled pattern.

Fine-Grained Enamels for Overpainting Lusters

Painting enamels, lusters, overglaze and underglaze require special firing procedures, to be detailed later.

Enamel Lumps as Jewels

Lumps of transparent enamel, premelted into glistening enamel "jewels" and incorporated into a design, are a comparatively recent development. They have been utilized with varying degrees of expertise. There is a limitless design potential in the little jewels as craftsmen begin to succeed in applying them to vertical surfaces.

Deep bowl. Polly Rothenberg. Mikado-red exterior, black crackle over flux interior. Collection of Mr. and Mrs. Herbert Tepping.

METALS

Copper

The metal most commonly used for enameling is pure 18-gauge copper. It is malleable, attractive, and inexpensive. For pieces that will be etched before they are enameled, a good weight is 16-gauge. Many enamelists prefer the lighter-weight 20-gauge metal for jewelry. Enamel fuses to copper at a temperature well below the metal's melting point of 1981° F. Copper is available in sheets, rolls, and attractive preformed basic shapes. Tubing, in several sizes, is stocked by most hardware stores; copper pipe up to about four inches in diameter can be purchased at plumbing supply shops. The pipe can be sliced for very effective use in forming footed bowls. A pipe cutter is a handy tool to own. Sometimes a plumbing shop will cut the pipe for you.

Preenameled Steel Tiles

Steel squares and rectangles in various sizes are available precoated on both sides with a base coat of fired enamel. They are comparatively inexpensive. Firing temperatures are the same as for copper.

Silver-Coated Steel Shapes

Small jewelry shapes and a few preformed small bowls in silver-coated steel are available in some enamel supply shops. These pieces must not be smoothed with a carborundum stone or steel wool. Any abrasive would remove the thin coating of silver. Firing temperatures are 1350° F. to 1450° F.

Silver

Fine silver (pure silver) in 18- to 20-gauge is preferred over sterling for enameling because there is no oxidation problem between firings. Fine silver is softer than sterling, but because it is easily deformed, the thinner gauges are not practical except for very delicate jewelry. Fine silver has a melting point of 1761° F., well above the fusing temperatures of enamels. Sterling, which contains a copper alloy, will begin to deform at 1500° F. It tends to discolor enamels.

Gold

Fine gold has a melting point of 1945° F. It is hard, and repeated firings will not deform it. Because there is no problem of oxidation, it does not need to be cleaned between firings if the fingers are kept off the fired surface.

Foils

Pure gold and silver foils can be cut between layers of tracing paper or tissue for effective application over fired enamel. After they are fused, foils must be covered with transparent enamel and fired again.

Gold Leaf

Gold foil is sometimes mistakenly called gold leaf. Although both materials are pure gold, different techniques must be followed in their application to enamel. Gold leaf is available as a thin film of gold adhered to a tissue backing sheet. Meticulous care must be exercised in applying and firing it to enamels.

Wire

Gold, silver, and copper wire, round, flat, and square, can be embedded in enameled surfaces for unusual effects.

Aluminum *

Porcelain enamel on aluminum is an important material in architectural and related industries, although aluminum is not widely used by many amateur enamel craftsmen. Aluminum has a *much lower melting point* than that of copper, steel, silver, and gold, which are the metals most in use by the enamel craftsman. It is necessary to use the correct aluminum alloy for enameling. Unlike pure copper, which has a constant melting temperature, some aluminum alloys melt below enameling temperature, while others will not fuse to enamel. The novice might consider 3003 for experimentation where only *one* firing is planned, as it requires no pretreatment other than assuring a chemically clean surface. This may be achieved by scouring with a cleaning powder such as Ajax or by burn-off at 1000° F. However, when multiple firings are involved, 6061 is recommended because the more common alloys, such as 3003 and 1100 will cause hairline cracks in the enamel upon repeated firings.

Aluminum enamels are different from those made for other metals; they must fuse at *lower* temperatures. Aluminum enamels are supplied to the enameler in clear frit form. Color is achieved by adding inorganic color oxides to the mill formula. They are ground into water suspension in a porcelain-lined ball mill to a fine-mesh slip (as fine as 325-mesh). Mill formulations, methods of application, and information on specific enamels are worked out with the frit supplier, then tested by the enameler. At present, spraying is the chief method of application. Spraying must be done in a spray booth equipped with an exhaust fan. The sprayed enamel is fired wet in an enameling furnace at 1000° F. for approximately seven minutes; length of firing time is important.

---

* Information by courtesy of The Ferro Corporation, Cleveland, Ohio.

Respiratory protection is indicated during operations because of airborne contamination from spraying, toxic metal fumes emanating from the firing oven, and fumes from pickling the metal, where it is acid-cleaned. However, in general, a spray booth with an adequate exhaust will provide sufficient protection from airborne contamination, and a well-ventilated room will take care of the fumes from pretreatment, in the case of small pieces enameled by the average craftsman who would like to experiment on a limited scale. The most important health consideration is to wash your hands after handling the raw materials.

Although the facilities required for enameling aluminum are not accessible to the average enamel craftsman, the potter who mixes his own clay and glazes may have most of the equipment necessary for preparing and enameling this metal.

Unsuitable Metals

Brass, bronze, pewter, and other high-content zinc and tin alloys are not appropriate for enameling; zinc and tin have very low melting points, and they will bubble under high temperatures, leaving ugly pits in the alloy metals. Gold and silver alloys have low melting points and are also unsatisfactory for enameling.

TOOLS AND EQUIPMENT

For Preparing Metal

The tools necessary for cutting and shaping metal pieces are simple and basic. Most of them can be bought in hardware stores. Copper sheet is usually cut with *metal shears*. Silver and gold sheet are cut with a *jeweler's saw*. Coarse to fine *files* remove rough edges and refine the shape. Fine *emery cloth* gives the entire piece a final polishing. *Steel wool* may be used to polish copper. A shallow bowl shape is formed on a *sandbag* or *wooden starting block* by means of a wooden or rawhide *mallet*. Copper can be hammered with a metal *hammer* on a flat surface. Curved shapes are formed over *steel stakes*.

For Applying Enamels

The required tools for application of enamels are absurdly simple; many of them can be found in the dime store. *Atomizers,* 80-mesh screen *sifters, spatulas, brushes,* and *tongs* are minimum requirements. The sprayers can be ordinary throat atomizers or aerosol spray units and electric sprayers, suitable for finely overspraying metal shapes with enameling gum or agar before the enamel is applied. Enamel is sifted over the gummed surface with screen sifters. Clean metal can be wet-packed with moist enamels by using a tiny *spatula* and a pointed tool or small brush. Painting enamels are applied with small fine *brushes*. Pieces can be dipped into liquid enamels, such as crackles and flux, with a pair of copper or wooden *tongs*.

Equipment and Tools for Firing Enamels

The major investment in enameling equipment is in the *kiln*, which is an oven for firing enamels. Some manufacturers offer a wide variety of sizes and types of enameling kilns. Those most in use in this country are electric. Many of them can be plugged directly into regular household receptacles. It is well to have them wired to a separate fuse box so that other electrical equipment does not draw off the current and cause an uneven firing. A kiln with steel exterior and adequate insulation will efficiently seal in the heat. Firing-chamber walls of high temperature refractory hold and evenly distribute heat. Doors may be pulldown, slide-down, or side-opening. However, it is possible to have a door rehung, if you decide that you would like to change the door of a particular kiln.

Although jewelry hobbyists make extensive use of small tabletop jewelry kilns, those persons who enjoy the craft to the

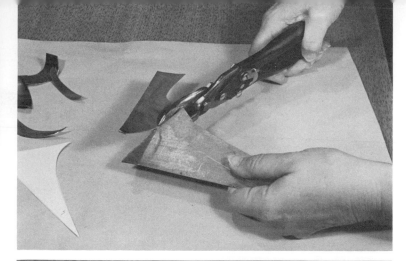

Copper is cut with metal shears.

Intricate designs are cut with a jeweler's saw.

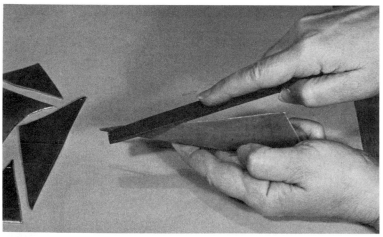

Heavy files smooth raw metal edges. If hand-held, the file is held diagonally to the edge. Keep files clean with a wire brush.

Edges of silver jewelry pieces are held in a vise. Jaws are protected by tape to avoid deep jaw marks.

Many sizes and types of stilts and trivets support enameled pieces in the kiln.

Fine firing racks for supporting inverted bowls are made by wiring clay plate pins to a mesh rack with nichrome wire.

A free-form shape is supported by steel-tipped star stilts and button stilts. When the piece has fired and cooled, these stilts are gently tapped loose.

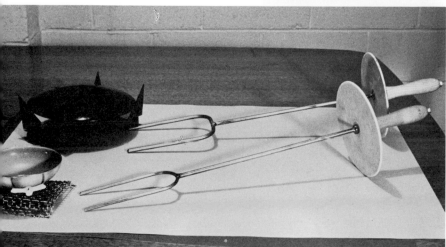

It is essential to have two sizes of firing forks: a narrow one for transporting small trivets to and from the kiln, and a wide one to hold a wide trivet or firing rack adequately.

extent that they find they want to make larger pieces, such as bowls, trays, wall panels, or enameled sculptures, soon feel the need of a larger kiln. It is suggested that, for the serious craftsman, a regular front-loading kiln, equipped with a pyrometer (heat indicator), be the initial investment. A top-loading kiln will not work because of the problem of removing a piece from the hot kiln. Unlike pottery, enameled pieces are placed in a hot kiln and removed from a hot kiln.

If the kiln has a kiln shelf over the floor element, it should be given three coats of kiln wash before it is put to use. Then if any enamel falls to the shelf, and melts, it can easily be cleaned away by scraping it off and then patching the scraped areas with additional kiln wash. Mix the dry wash powder with water to the consistency of thin cream. First, brush the shelf with water. Then, with long strokes, quickly brush on the wash in one direction until the entire shelf is covered. Keep the brush full and flowing. Load the brush again and apply a second coat in a crosswise direction. Apply a third coat cross-wise to the second coat (parallel to the first coat). It is important to let the kiln wash dry *slowly* for two or three days. If the kiln has no floor element, enamel-covered pieces on trivets will probably be set directly on the kiln floor when they are fired. Fill any cracks in the floor with kiln cement mixed to a paste. When the cement has dried, prepare the floor surface with kiln wash as described for the kiln shelf. Crumbs of firebrick, dried wash particles, or flecks of enamel should be kept off the elements. A vacuum cleaner with a crack-cleaning attachment is a handy tool for cleaning up stray particles. Good housekeeping in both enameling and firing is essential for best results.

Basic enamel-firing accessories are nichrome mesh *firing racks*, various sizes of *trivets* and *steel-tipped star stilts* (not the all-clay ones) for supporting pieces in the kiln, two sizes of *firing forks,* asbestos or *transite board,* and *asbestos mittens*. Accessories for firing enamels should be of Monel Metal or stainless steel. (Tools are illustrated throughout the book.)

Small table-top kilns are useful for firing jewelry pieces and small convex trays that will not be counterenameled. Pieces are inserted with a small spatula. The top is removable. Courtesy of American Art Clay Co.

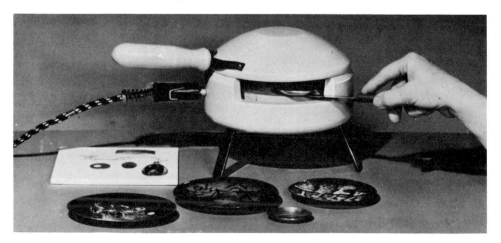

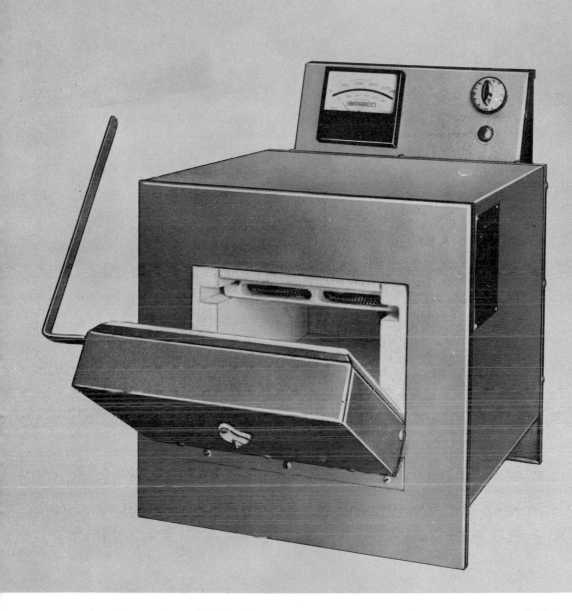

An adequate large kiln has insulated steel construction, fire chamber walls of high-temperature refractory, and is equipped with a pyrometer. Courtesy of American Art Clay Co.

Methods

PREPARATION

Forming a Simple Copper Shape

The formation of a shallow hammered-copper tray requires a piece of flat copper, usually 18-gauge, a firmly packed canvas or leather bag of sand, a forming hammer (a ball peen hammer will do), and a leather mallet. If the piece is to be a round one, a wooden starting block can be used. Cut out the shape with metal shears, then flatten the edge with the leather mallet. To refine the edge, stroke it diagonally away from you with a fairly large file. File from the tip to the handle of the file with a light touch and a regular rhythm until you have removed unwanted projections.

For a first free-form piece, place the cut and prepared flat shape on the sandbag and strike a very light blow to the center of the piece. Working in concentric paths, and following the shape of the tray, each light blow should just cover the edge of the preceding one until you reach ¼-inch from the edge. If the very edge of the copper is hammered, it may thin too much, and possibly split. From time to time, invert the piece and tap it all over to even the rim. Repeat the routine until you have a nice shallow form.

If you want a fairly smooth surface, planish the metal by tapping it with the leather mallet over a slightly rounded steel stake. However, a hammered tray that shows all the tool marks through sparkling transparent enamel can be an object of great beauty. A spun, preformed shape can be hammered for a similar effect.

A wooden starting block can be made from a section of hardwood log that has a shallow saucer-shaped depression ground or gouged into one end-grained surface. Or a small block can be made by a carpenter in a woodworking shop; a six-inch cube of hardwood, such as oak or birch, is put on a lathe, and a shallow saucer-shaped depression is ground into one *end-grained* surface. The depression can also be gouged out with sharp tools. Three or four inches in diameter will be adequate. Steel doming blocks are sold by some metalcraft supply houses. They have several sizes of small depressions especially suitable for forming jewelry shapes.

Cut a cardboard shape a little larger than the planned tray. Lay it flat on copper sheet and score around it with a metal scriber.

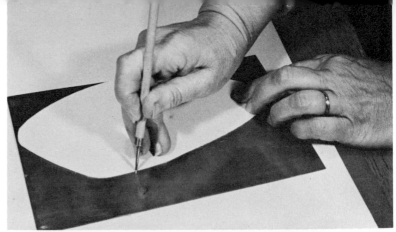

Cut out the shape with metal snips. If the copper curls, flatten it with a leather mallet.

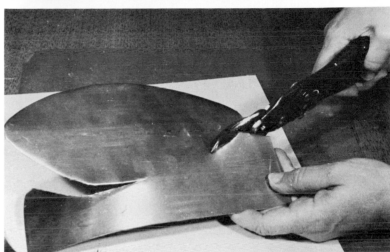

With a round-faced forming hammer, work all over the shape each time around, and sink it gradually.

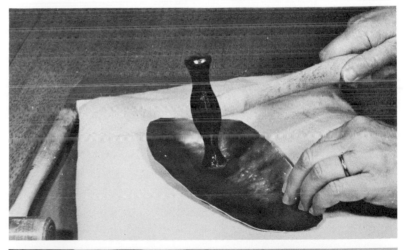

On a forming block, sink the disk in the center, then turn the disk as you pound it in concentric circles from center to edge.

Smooth the tray with a leather mallet or planishing hammer by light tapping on a slightly rounded steel stake. Anneal the metal if it stiffens. Grasp the hammer handle with the fist or with one finger extended to control light tapping.

A rubber wheel impregnated with abrasive is fine for smoothing raw metal edges. Start the motor; with a sharp instrument, cut a groove in the abrasive wheel as it rotates. Do not hold the edge of a piece in one spot, or the abrasive will cut a "scallop." Move the edge up and down. Hold the piece in the position shown, but not above the edge of the wheel closest to you, or the piece will be flung from your hands.

Discolorations can be removed with Sparex solution or a solution of one part nitric acid to eight parts water.

Annealing

Pounding and working metal will stiffen it because of the mangling of the molecular structure of the metal. If it is heated to high temperature, the metal becomes malleable again. From time to time, as it is worked, the copper piece must be heated red-hot, then cooled. This process is called *annealing*. It is important to anneal the metal frequently to keep it soft enough so that only light blows of the hammer are required to move and stretch it.

Removing Firescale

Each time copper is annealed, it will oxidize. Firescale will form on the bare metal. To clean off the scale, submerge the metal in a deep Pyrex dish of Sparex #2 solution until it turns a clean copper-pink; then rinse it well. For the solution, dissolve two and a half pounds of dry Sparex in seven pints of warm water. This should make a gallon of solution. Keep it in a covered crock or glass container. An alternate method of controlling firescale is to paint the copper with a commercial firescale inhibitor, such as Amacote or Scale-off, *before* it is annealed. Firescale will peel off in sheets when the piece has been removed from the kiln and begins to cool. The scale remover must be dried before it is put into the kiln.

Paint metal with scale inhibitor before annealing it.

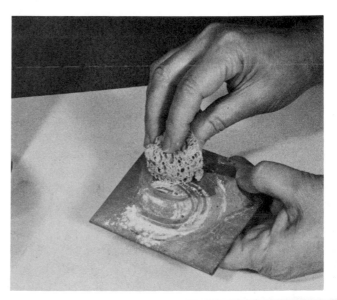

Copper can be cleaned by scrubbing it with scouring powder. Rinse it well.

APPLICATION OF ENAMEL

Counterenameling

When the copper piece is clean, it is time to plan the first coat of enamel, which will be applied to the *underside* of your piece. This first layer of enamel will brace a *shallow* copper shape against flexing or contracting of the metal when the enamel on the top surface is fired. It will equalize (or counter) the top surface tensions and prevent cracks from forming in the enamel. This first coat of enamel applied to the underneath surface is referred to as *counterenamel,* although it is not any special kind of enamel. It may even be the same kind and color that is applied to the top surface.

If square and rectangular trays and bowls are not counterenameled *before* the top surface is enameled, there will be a splintering of enamel at the corners almost immediately, while it is cooling. However, a deep, concave round shape has little tendency to flex and eventually crack the top-side enamel if it is not counterenameled. The metal can be left bare and painted with *glaze surfacer* to retard tarnishing, in this case.

Sometimes odd scraps of enamels are collected together in a jar and used for counterenamel or so-called *backing enamel* on the underneath sides of tiles and panels that will be cemented down and concealed. However, it is wise to select the counterenamel for bowls and trays with as much discrimination as that used in selecting colors for the top surfaces.

When you have selected an enamel color for counterenameling your piece, paint the top surface (which will not yet be enameled) with a liquid firescale inhibitor, such as Scale-off or Amacote, which protects the bare copper from accumulating a crust of heavy firescale when the counterenamel is fired. If the counterenamel is regular 80-mesh dry granular enamel, it is applied by the *dusting method.*

Dusting or Sifting Enamels

Sifted dry enamels must be applied over an adhesive that holds the powder in place while it is firing in the kiln. The adhesive used for projects in this book, unless otherwise noted, is a solution of one of the commercial enameling gums or liquid agar, in the proportion of one part gum or agar to three parts water. This consistency will go through a sprayer without sputtering or clogging. The solution can be applied with an atomizer, an aerosol spray unit, or an electric sprayer. If you find that a commercial enameling gum has a tendency to sputter, try adding some liquid agar to the solution. For a small, flat piece, such as a jewelry shape, apply the gum with a small soft brush. Gum is also brushed on for application of silver or gold foil and gold leaf, as well as for a few other decorating methods that will be discussed in the appropriate sections. Where more than one layer of sifted enamel is applied *before* the firing, a sprayer must be used. Gum cannot be brushed over a coat of unfired enamel.

Before the sifting begins, place before you a stack of several loose sheets of paper, such as magazine pages. When the enamel is dusted, much of it will fall free of the piece and accumulate on the top paper. As soon as a new color is to be applied, the top sheet can be lifted off and bent to form a pouring groove so the accumulation of fallen grains can be returned to its jar. If the paper is still clean, it can be reused. If it is soiled, discard it, and you have the next sheet already in place. It is advisable to spread a newspaper beside you and hold the copper shape over this paper for gum spraying. If spraying is done over loose enamel, it will dampen unused enamel and make it unfit for sifting until it dries again.

Begin at the edge of a piece and spray either in concentric paths toward the center or in pie-shaped sections. With an 80-mesh screen sifter, dust enamel thinly and evenly over the gummed area, beginning at the

To apply liquid adhesive, hold the piece at arm's length and spray lightly all over. If it is held too close, the gum will puddle and run. Keep bare fingers off the clean metal.

edge, *which will dry out first*. Spray another section and sift enamel over it; repeat this routine until the entire surface is covered with a thin sifting of enamel. (The complete operation is repeated twice more; then the entire surface is given a final spraying with gum.) There should now be three thin even coats of enamel. Edges are inspected; any bare or thinly covered spots should be dusted and sprayed again. Then the piece is set on a trivet near the kiln, and left to dry.

Wet inlay

Wet inlay, or wet charging, as it is also called, is the process of applying moist, finely ground enamels with a tiny spatula or brush. This method is especially suitable for application of enamels in techniques such as cloisonné, champlevé, and plique-à-jour, as well as application over metal foils and for some Limoges-type designs. Although the enamels can be applied in an 80-mesh grind,

the result will be equally interesting if they are ground finer by means of a mortar and pestle. It is advisable to wash enamels before wet-pack application. Because the enamel is applied thicker than when it is sifted, transparents will appear less brilliant, and opaques might show whitish rings around each application, if this washing is neglected.

To wash enamels, place some of the enamel in a glass jar and run water into it. The swirling water will become cloudy. Let it settle for several seconds; then pour off the cloudy water. Repeat this procedure until the water becomes clear. When enamel colors have been washed, they can be dried on top of the kiln and stored in closed containers ready for use. If they sit unused for a considerable length of time, they may need to be rewashed before being used for wet inlay (wet charge). If you are washing enamels in preparation for wet inlay, put the separate moist colors into small individual

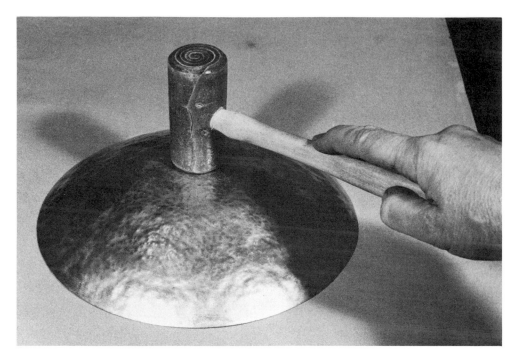

A spun bowl is hammered all over. Magazines make good hammering surfaces for this kind of texturing. Hammer the top surface, then turn the piece over and flatten the base with a leather mallet.

File rough places from the edge. Make long, even strokes in one direction, going from tip to handle of the file.

Rub the surface all over to smooth it. Steel wool should be used in an area away from enamels.

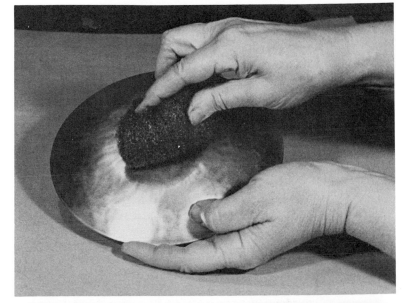

Scale inhibitor is painted over the bare metal before it is annealed. Let it dry completely before it is fired.

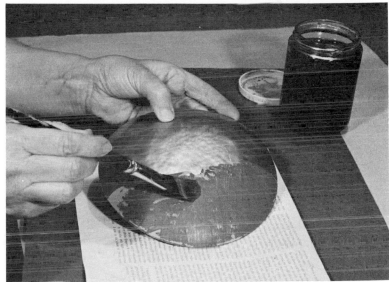

When the piece is removed from the kiln, firescale and scale inhibitor peel off in sheets as the piece cools.

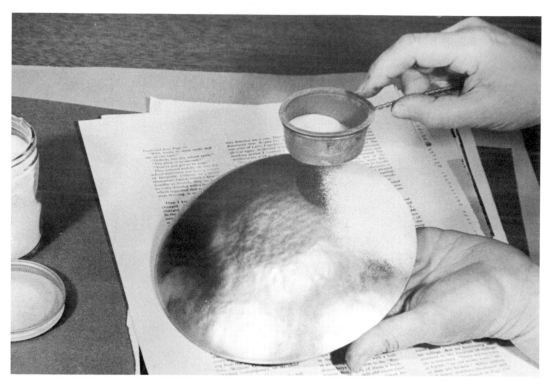

Spray the surface in sections, and apply sifted enamel, beginning at the rim.

The piece is fired upside down on a sturdy trivet.

When flux has been fired to both sides of the bowl, transparent garnet red is fired on the bowl's interior. Garnet red transparent lumps are fired last.

containers. Glass coasters are fine for holding some of each separate color that will be used in a design. Blend a few drops of gum solution with the moist enamel.

Scoop up a small amount of wet enamel with a tiny spoon-shaped spatula and push it into place in the design either with a pointed instrument or with a small brush. Pack it well into the corners of the areas it will cover; then pat it flat. A drop of water touched to it from the end of a small watercolor brush will flatten it out and carry the enamel into crevices that may be difficult to reach. When one wet-charged color area is laid against an area of another color, care must be taken to align the adjoining edges evenly and not leave an unplanned ragged juncture. Pick up and pack one enamel color, then pat it smooth; draw off excess moisture by touching the wet enamel with a tissue or a small piece of soft blotter. Next, the adjoining color is laid in, moisture is

drawn off, and the two areas are gently pushed together with the back of the little spatula. This procedure is continued until the design is completed. It is a slow and exacting process, although historically it was the chief method of applying enamels.

Dipping

Enamels such as liquid flux can be applied to both sides of a small shape at the same time by the dipping method. Liquid enamel must be stirred each time that it is used because it tends to settle thickly in the bottom of a container. Pour some of the liquid flux into a small broad vessel. Grasp the copper shape firmly with narrow tongs and lower it into the enamel until it is completely immersed. If the enamel is the correct consistency (like thick cream), a thin coating will cling to the metal surface. Give the piece a slight shake to remove excess enamel, then lay it over a wire rack to dry. A very

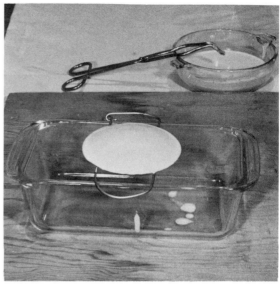

A copper piece is dipped into liquid enamel with metal tongs.

Wire from a coat hanger can be constructed to form a drying rack.

good drying rack can be formed from part of a bent wire coat hanger. If one enamel coat seems too thin, when the piece is partially dry, dip it in the liquid a second time, taking care not to disturb the first coat. When the enamel has completely dried, fire it at 1500° F. until it is shiny. This is an easy way to apply base coats of enamel to small pieces for quantity production.

Sprayed Enamel

Although finely ground enamels can be suspended in a thin solution of diluted gum and sprayed over metal shapes, this must be done in a spray booth equipped with an exhaust fan to draw off toxic spray mist, which can cause harm to the lungs. The enamel should be ground to 200-mesh or *finer*, and the diluted gum solution would be about six parts water to one part commercial gum or agar. Spraying is commonly done in commercial production of utility enameled ware.

Amateur craftsmen would do well to avoid this method of application.

FIRING ENAMELS

Preparing the Piece for Firing

When a piece has been covered with enamel and gum, it must be completely dried before it is put into the kiln. If it should still be damp, the moisture will turn into steam in the heat of the kiln. This is especially disastrous for a steep-sided shape; the loosened enamel may fall to the floor of the kiln and become a molten mass. When the enamel appears dry and feels crusty to the touch of a fingertip, the piece is ready for the kiln. If there is room to slide a firing fork under the trivet, it can be set into the kiln without a mesh firing rack. With the enamel-covered piece in place, lift the trivet with a firing fork, open the kiln door, and set the trivet into the center of the kiln as quickly as possible without disturbing the enamel. The door must be closed at once so that little heat is lost. Asbestos gloves should be worn whenever the kiln door is opened.

The Firing Process

If the kiln is really hot, 1600° F. to 1700° F. or hotter, the temperature will not drop too low when the door is opened. It will build up again quickly after the door is closed. Temperature in the kiln can be lowered by "fanning" the door, if the kiln gets too hot while a piece is firing. The door should be opened *only an inch or two* and fanned back and forth to lower the heat. In general, a good firing temperature for most opaques and transparents in 80-mesh enamel, except in special instances, is 1500° F.

When a piece has fired for about two to three minutes, the door should be held ajar for *just an instant* so the firing process can be observed. When the piece becomes a bright red and the enamel appears shiny and nearly smooth, it is removed from the kiln. With hands protected by asbestos mitts, slide the firing fork under the trivet or firing rack, remove the piece carefully, and set it on a heatproof surface so it may cool *slowly*. An asbestos or transite board is a fine cooling surface. Although the enamel may not be completely flat, it will get smoother with each subsequent firing. Never put the hot piece under water to fast-cool it. Tiny hairline cracks may form in the fired enamel surface even though it appears to be unbroken. When the piece is refired, water that may be trapped in these cracks will form steam during a later firing, and bits of enamel can pop loose in the kiln and ruin a carefully wrought design.

During the firing process, the kiln door must not be opened more than a crack for two very good reasons. The more obvious reason is that the temperature may drop too low. The other reason is one that is sometimes overlooked by some very experienced enamelists. When enamel begins to fire, first it turns black; then it starts to melt and draw up into pockmarked little balls. *At this point,* some bare metal is exposed between the tiny enamel nodules before the melting enamel softens and spreads over it again. If a blast of cool air from the open kiln door should strike the exposed metal *at this time*, firescale will form quickly and will likely interrupt the normal fusing process. All sorts of aggravations can result. The enamel may leave most of these scaly spots completely bare; pits can form; discolorations may occur in the enamel; or partly fired lumps may congeal and stubbornly resist later firings.

Special firing instructions are given in succeeding pages where special problems are encountered, such as for steep-sided bowls, lusters, and overglazes, crackle enamels, and others.

Pitting of Enamels During Firing

Bubbling and pitting, the bane of the novice enameler, has many causes.

The metal may not be pure. For enameling, it is wise to secure metal from a reliable supplier. An inferior grade may continually emit gases, no matter how well it is cleaned. These gases blow holes in the firing enamel, and leave little pits.

The enamel may be dirty or of inferior grade. Avoid purchasing enamel from unreliable sources.

The metal surface may not be clean of all traces of grease and soil. All metal should be cleaned just before it is enameled. Let it be "hospital clean"!

The enamel may still be damp when put into the kiln. Rising steam will blow holes and cause pits.

The enamel may be too thinly applied.

The piece may be underfired, either at too low a temperature or for too short a time.

Some Firing Characteristics of Certain Colors

The following are notes on the author's own experience with various colors. Each enamel craftsman will discover favorite colors, and learn their individual properties.

Flux

Low-firing flux is useful where flow is desired. It makes a good base enamel on inclined surfaces that will be overfired, and it facilitates movement and blending of colors over it. Crackle patterns are enhanced by a covering coat of medium flux. Applied as a thin topcoat over stubborn high-fire opaques, such as beige, it helps flatten them. Where ugly cracks have formed in some opaques, a thin sifting of soft flux fired over the top will remedy this problem and not degrade the color. When a piece is fired several times, a sifting of flux around the edges between firings will protect edges from burning out.

Liquid Flux

Liquid flux is ground to finer mesh than 80. It does not always fire clear in the first firing. Subsequent firings give it a metallic iridescence if fired on bare copper. It is useful for rolling around the interior of narrow tubular shapes. Liquid flux should not be put into a pickling solution. It will become dull and crusty.

White

By itself, white resembles porcelain china. A good firing temperature for whites, except for hard white, is 1400° F. If over-fired, white turns light green in areas. A second or third thin coat should remedy this. Soft white under transparents will bubble through and give interesting texture.

Opalescent White

Over a flux base, opalescent white is very delicate. Fire it at 1400° F. for true opalescence. It may become dull if it is left too long in the pickling bath. It is effective in portraits.

Black

When patching black, do not use the wet-inlay method. It will leave a cloudy ring around the patched area. Paint the patch spot with squeegee oil; sift on a thin layer of black enamel; then spray the entire black area and sift a thin layer of black over it. Fire in one firing. Blacks should not be left too long in a pickling bath; they tend to become dulled.

Brown

Transparent browns, fired directly on copper at 1500° F. for several firings, are quite handsome. They are especially fine combined with transparent yellow or over opaque yellow and beige. Saddle brown is a terra-cotta brown opaque. Cordova is lighter, and combines well with yellow and orange. If overfired, browns in the opaques will form black areas. The opaques must not be left too long in pickle bath; they will lose some gloss.

Yellow

The lighter tones and citrous yellows are quite nice, especially with a coat of flux fired *over them*. Opalescent yellow fired over a *fired* coat of *soft flux* will form fascinating brownish areas with streaks of brown and yellow. This is most exciting on inclined surfaces where it can flow slightly. Golden-yellow transparent is the color "most likely

Round panel. Mary Sharp. Design was traced onto bare copper. Enamels were mixed with ½ water and ½ liquid gum solution, and applied with a brush as smoothly as possible, for this unusual effect. Courtesy of the artist.

HI THERE. Elinor Helitzer. Transparent and opaque enamels were sifted, wet-packed, and sgraffitoed to achieve the design. Colors are gold, coral pink, black, and gray-greens. 8 inches by 12 inches. Courtesy of the artist.

to succeed." It almost never fails as a base coat over copper. If fired lower than 1500° F., it may form attractive reddish areas. Subsequent higher firings will gradually eliminate these areas. To retain them, keep additional firings at 1400° F. Amber yellow does best applied in two thin coats over flux.

Reds

Reds cause the novice more concern than almost any other color, and with good reason. Transparent reds fired directly over copper are difficult to fire clear. They have a distressing tendency to dull and become opaque. Over flux, they are disappointingly light unless several coats are thinly applied, not too hot. Opaque reds will form black areas with the first firing. Add one or more coats with firings in between. Transparent red over any opaque red is a rich, handsome color. *Brick* red opaque is dark and most attractive. It should be used more often.

Pink

Transparent pink is delicate over flux or opaque white. It is disappointing over bare copper, turns gold over silver or silver foil. For a surprisingly lovely effect, fire flux, then a coat of transparent pink, then, at 1450° F., a layer of opalescent pink.

Purple

A real royal purple is hard to find. Most transparent purples look well over flux. Fire two thin coats.

Blues

The most satisfying, stable, and popular colors are the entire range of blues, both transparent and opaque. All the blue opaques look vibrant with light blue or light turquoise transparent over them. The kiln door should not be opened during early firing stages of blue enamels because these colors tend to "ball up" more than the other colors,

and firescale can form between the small humps and discolor the blue. When transparent dark blues and turquoise are fired over bare copper, they will show most vibrancy if fired several times at about 1500° F. The opaques: Delft, Wedgwood, Indian, peacock, and porcelain are among the most satisfying of all enamel colors, and they combine very well with white, red, and orange opaques. They are especially handsome when *over*fired over soft flux on a steep-sided bowl.

Transparent Smoke Gray

This interesting color is the nearest to transparent black. When applied on bare copper in thick and thin areas and fired at 1500° F. it resembles a tortoiseshell. It will turn putty color over silver, however.

Transparent Champagne

Champagne is a light honey-color enamel. It is attractive fired hot (1550° F.) over bare copper, and combines well with opaque blues.

ENAMELING STEEP-SIDED SHAPES

When a flat or shallow metal shape is enameled and fired, gravity holds the enamel in place even though it may be loosely applied. However, all conditions must be favorable when a steep-sided piece is fired, in order to prevent the enamel from falling off in patches. Anyone who enjoys enamelwork should be able to enamel one of these pieces successfully by following a few necessary precautions.

The first step is to clean the copper shape thoroughly, then paint the inside surface with scale remover to control the formation of firescale. When it has dried, spray an even coat of diluted gum over a wedge-shaped section of the bowl's exterior surface.

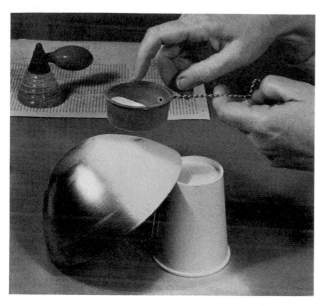

Tap the sifter lightly with hand relaxed. Keep plenty of enamel in the sifter so it dusts evenly.

Lower the bowl carefully onto the firing rack with the narrow firing fork. When withdrawing the fork, take care to avoid striking the bowl edge and the enamel.

Prop the inside edge of the bowl on an inverted paper cup so the side of the bowl is nearly horizontal. Immediately sift a thin coat of enamel evenly over the wet gummed section, beginning at the edge, or rim, which will dry out first, and working toward the base. If the gum begins to dry before it is covered with enamel, apply more gum. Because this first coat anchors the enamel to the copper shape, it must be applied carefully. Continue the process, rotating the shape until wedge-shaped areas of gum and enamel are applied all the way around. When the outside is completely covered, repeat the process *twice more*. Each thin coating of enamel is alternated with a sprayed coat of gum; then the piece is examined to make sure there are no thin areas where a glint of copper shows through. Spray a final coat of gum solution over the entire surface. Place the bowl upside down to dry. Ceramic plate pins wired to a mesh firing rack with nichrome wire make a good support for the firing of inverted bowls. To avoid unnecessary rehandling, put the piece directly on the firing rack to dry.

Enamel should always dry thoroughly and slowly before a piece is put into the kiln. If it is subjected, even for an instant, to hot temperature while it is still damp, rising steam will cause an upheaval in the enamel and loosen it. When the piece is fired, the metal flexes and any loosened areas of dry enamel fall off the sides and onto the kiln floor. When the enamel has dried in a warm place for a half hour or longer, it may be touched very lightly to test whether it is dry. Touch it on a horizontal plane so that if you should disturb the enamel, it will not drop off. When it is dry, it should feel crusty. Fire it at about 1500° F. The enamel is mature when it turns a bright red in the kiln. Remove the bowl from the kiln and cool it slowly. If enamel is left too long in the kiln, it tends to flow downward and form a thick rim on the bowl's edge. When the piece has cooled, clean the inside surface thoroughly.

Starting with the edge, cover wedge-shaped sections in thin layers, spraying after each section is dusted.

Use the largest star stilt that will fit the bottom of the bowl. Position it on the stilt near the kiln so it does not have to be transported very far.

Obviously, the bowl cannot be propped on a paper cup while the interior enamel is applied. With a little practice, the shape can be held in one hand while gum and enamel are applied with the other hand. Some enamel craftsmen leave a bare spot on the outside base of a bowl so they can set it on a small clay disk while it is fired. If the exterior is *completely* covered with fired enamel, a different type of trivet must be used. Steel-pronged star stilts are available in several sizes. To deter the bowl from sliding off the stilt when it is transported to the kiln, roughen the bottom of the bowl with an abrasive stone. Removing the glossiness of the enamel will also help prevent the bowl from sliding off the stilt while it is being positioned in the kiln. When the fired piece is removed from the hot kiln, take care that it does not topple off the trivet. After the

piece has cooled, the star stilt can easily be tapped loose from the base of the bowl. If a final firing is done with the piece in an inverted position, stilt marks melt away. Some enamelists hesitate to fire a bowl upside down, but this can be done very safely if the temperature is correct and if the piece is not left unattended while it is firing; it must be removed from the kiln at the very moment the stilt marks turn shiny. To leave it longer would allow the molten enamel to flow downward and possibly form a thickened rim on the inverted bowl.

It is more difficult to apply enamel to a tall narrow shape. For the interior surface, liquid flux can be poured in, rolled around, then poured out again. If you want color on the inside, dust a colored enamel over the wet flux before firing both coats together, at 1500° F.

Soft-stencil stripes applied in shades of brown and orange over beige as described under "Stencil Enamels," Section 4. Dark brown transparent enamel interior.

For cup shape, roll liquid flux or liquid white around interior. Roll it quickly, then give it a slight shake. Color can be dusted lightly over it.

METHODS

Cup is supported on cardboard tube and rolled as enamel is applied.

Remove cup from tube with spatula and fingers. Set it directly on a firing rack.

Base coat was fired and second coat applied, sgraffitoed, and fired. Colors are dove gray over transparent brown, with transparent beige fired over all, at 1450° F.

Design Techniques

STENCIL ENAMELS

Stenciling is a simple and basic method of enriching the enameled surface of a tray, bowl, panel, or piece of jewelry. Stencils can also form a wealth of decorative effects when all their varied potentials are explored and developed. They can be used effectively alone or in combination with other decorative processes. They can set off areas of contrasting background color. In addition to soft and firm paper stencils, or friskets, almost anything that is flat and has an interesting shape will create texture patterns in small areas of larger designs. A working plan in color and to correct scale is very helpful.

Stencils can be cut from paper towels or from the paper filter disks used in drip-cone coffee makers. The latter are tough when they are wet, and do not overstretch as some kinds of paper towels may do. They hold up under repeated use. This quality is an asset when more than one piece in the same pattern is planned. A wet, soft-paper stencil laid flush against a fired enamel surface will form a sharply defined edge.

Gum is sprayed over the stencil and the enameled surface; then dry enamel is sifted over the stencil edges. Finally, the stencil is picked up by the edge with tweezers, and carefully removed. When it has dried, the piece is fired at 1450° F.

Frisket shapes cut from stiff paper can be held or propped slightly above the gummed surface. When enamel is sifted over the frisket from this elevated position, some of it drifts underneath the paper shape and creates a soft diffused edge. Combinations of sharp and soft edges make pleasing designs.

Frisket shapes cut from stiff paper can be held or propped slightly above the gummed enamel surface. When enamel is sifted from this position, some of it drifts underneath the stencil's edge, and creates a soft diffused effect.

Two simple abstract shapes are stenciled over a prefired base coat.

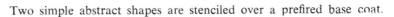

Where two colors overlap, they form a third color. Black overglaze
strokes complete the design.

Curved cardboard stencils are held
above a curved surface to form
diffused stripes.

Striped bowl. Polly Rothenberg. Shades of green transparent and opaque stripes over a gray base. Transparent champagne sifted over the exterior. Dark green transparent interior.

A straightedge held close to the surface will form one diffused edge and one sharp edge.

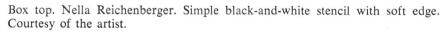
Stenciled decanters with sgraffito, overglaze, and liquid gold details.

Box top. Nella Reichenberger. Simple black-and-white stencil with soft edge.
Courtesy of the artist.

CRAB. Linda Gebert. Background of sifted transparents and opaques in green and blue, fired high. The crab is stenciled in reds and orange opaques, shaded and sgraffitoed. Foil and cloisonné "warts" on crab. Courtesy of the artist.

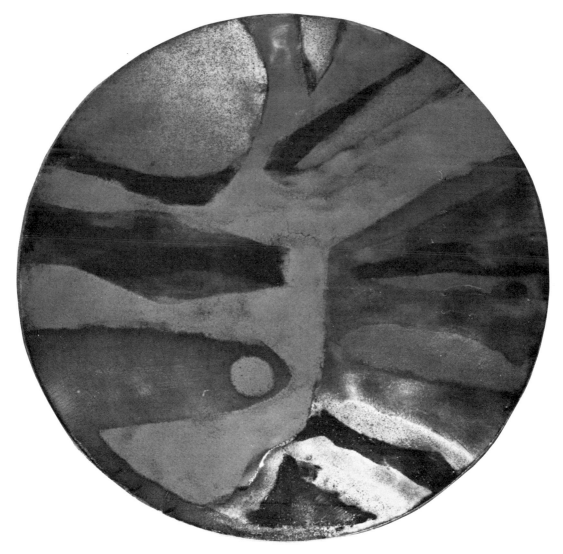

ABSTRACT RED. Linda Gebert. Combination of stenciled and wet-inlay colors in gold and red. Courtesy of the artist.

Found Objects as Stencils

Any number of "found objects," laid against an enameled surface, create unusual textures when dry enamel is sifted over them. Gum must be sprayed over the "stencil" object before it is removed with tweezers so that excess enamel clings to it instead of falling off and spoiling the design. Slices of sponge, braids, twigs, straws, and dried marine forms are some materials that come to mind. Possibilities are limited only by one's capacity for selection. Once the imagination has been freed from the traditional concept of stencils as cutout paper shapes laid flat against a surface, their decorative potentials become apparent.

In selecting materials for stenciling, keep in mind that only the flat, or profile, shape of an object will be transferred in enamel. Third dimension can be added by sifting or by the application of one, two, or more additional stencils. Cut away all parts of the objects that clutter their distinguishing features. The most interesting application of a found object is its incorporation into a larger or more complex composition. When possible, try to use it in a concept that is different from its original function. Netting can be used for texture rather than as *net* in a design. The dried bony spine of a fish can become a form of plant life; or a slice of dry seedpod may be just the shape to stencil the outlines of a horned marine creature!

Copper panel is given coats of transparent smoke-gray fired at 1550° F., on both sides. Slices of sponge and broom straws are positioned as stencils.

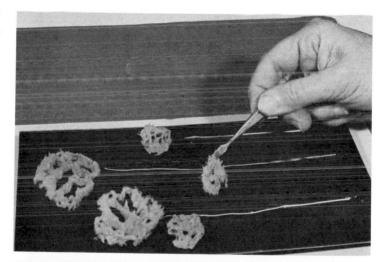

Enameling gum is sprayed overall, and white opaque enamel is sifted over the surface, with siftings thin around the edges. Stencils are removed.

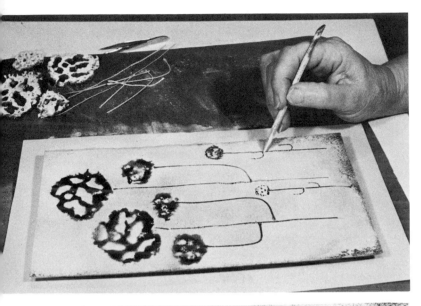

Additional lines are scratched (sgraffitoed) with a pointed tool.

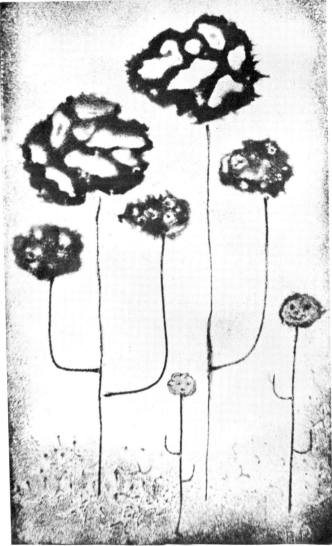

Some of the moist white enamel at the bottom of the panel is "dabbed" for texture. The panel is fired at 1450° F.

Gray and white opaque enamels are sifted over plant leaves and the dried spines of perch, which are positioned on a black enameled steel tile.

As each found object is removed with tweezers, more gray and white enamels are sifted lightly to make a shadow effect and snow.

WEEDS IN WINTER. Panel in black, white, and gray is mounted against rust-color burlap.

Stencil Designs on Bare Metal

When stencil designs are placed directly on bare copper rather than on a prefired enamel base surface, the effect is a raised champlevé with embossed enamel areas instead of a continuous level surface. It is effective for flat panels and for the exterior of steep-sided pieces that show the pattern to advantage. The contrast between rich matte softness of the metal and clear brilliance of the fired enamel is fully emphasized when edges of the enamel design are distinct rather than diffused.

If the copper piece is a flat tile or panel, there will be variations in surface tensions between the top and back sides of the panel if the underside is counterenameled too thickly. Enamel the backside lightly without being concerned whether it entirely covers.

It will be cemented down and concealed when it is completed. The enamel may be a little heavier in back of the surface stencil design.

For a purely decorative piece, it is not necessary to enamel the interior surface of a cup or tall vessel; its curved shape will prevent the piece from warping when it is fired. However, if the tall piece is to hold liquids, it is advisable to enamel the inside surface. Liquid flux is easily applied to it.

The first step is to clean and dry the cup's interior surface thoroughly. Roll liquid flux around the inside of the cup with a smooth rapid motion that covers the entire inside surface. A slight shake should remove the surplus enamel at the rim of the cup. Consistency of the liquid flux should be like thick cream. It should be stirred thoroughly from

The bare metal surface is sprayed with gum. Lengths of string and narrow strips of paper-towel stencils are applied with tweezers.

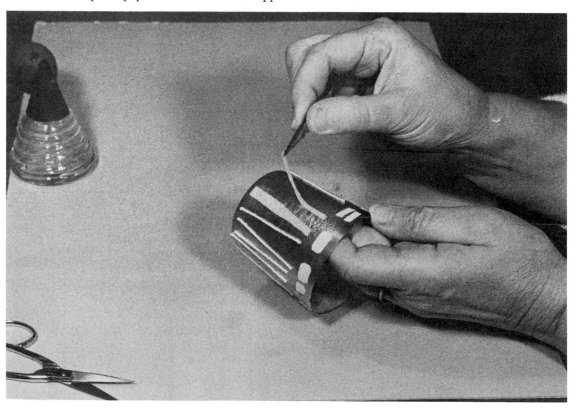

time to time because it tends to settle thickly in the bottom of the container. The cup is set aside and dried completely. Fire at 1500° F.

A characteristic of fired liquid flux is its tendency to shed some pulverized enamel when it is subjected to an acid or other pickling solution. It becomes dull and rough. But the exterior must be cleaned before it can be enameled. Set the cup in an upright position in an empty deep glass Pyrex dish; put a weight or stone inside the cup; and pour pickling solution into the dish until it comes nearly to the top of the cup but does not flow into it. After a few minutes of soaking, remove the cup, rinse it, and polish it with steel wool. Repeat the process until the cup's exterior is clean, smooth, and ready for enameling.

Enamel colors that are not injured by a pickling solution must be used for the exterior design. The cup's surface is sprayed with diluted gum solution, and stencils are applied and sprayed again. Enamel is sifted over the stencils and on the bottom of the cup. Remove the stencils carefully; count them to make sure none are missed. If a stencil is inadvertently left in place during the firing, it will leave a ragged little enamel bubble. Unfired enamel edges are straightened and refined with a tiny spatula, and stray grains of enamel are removed from the bare copper areas with a small damp brush. Place the piece directly on the firing rack to dry in an inverted position. When the enamel is completely dry, fire the cup at 1500° F. until the enamel is shiny. If it is overfired, heavy firescale will form on exposed metal areas and will be difficult to remove. Clean the cup and polish the bare copper.

String is wrapped around the cup over the vertical stencils. Small paper rectangles are positioned just below the cup's rim.

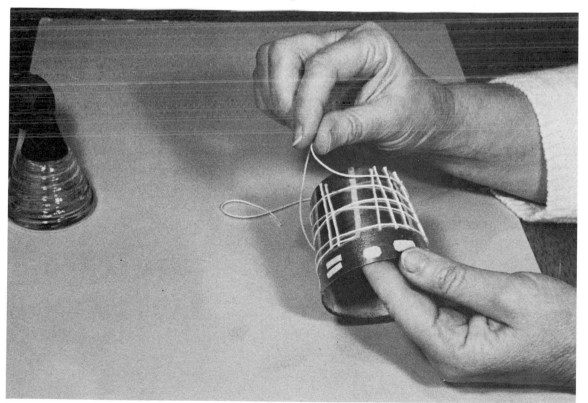

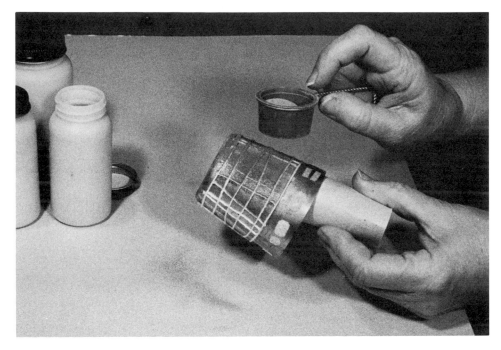

Gum is applied, and cerulean blue opaque is sifted over the entire exterior surface.

The cup is weighted with a stone. Pickle solution is poured nearly to the rim, but is not allowed to flow into the cup.

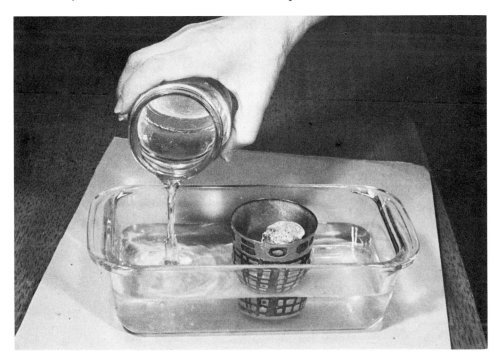

The cup is cleaned and polished; or bare metal areas can be oxidized.

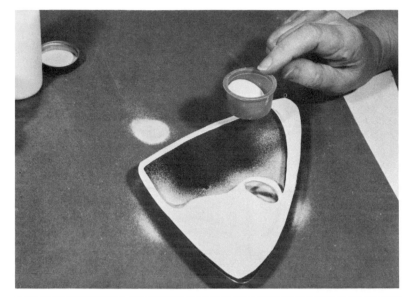

Walnut-brown transparent has been fired on both sides of a tray. The top surface is sprayed with diluted gum. A cardboard stencil is positioned so it rests on the rim of the tray. Ivory opaque and small amounts of colors are sifted over exposed areas. The tray is sprayed lightly and sifted again. The piece is dried.

Lines and broken lines are scribed with a sharp tool. Loosened enamel is dumped off, and the tray is fired until the enamel appears shiny.

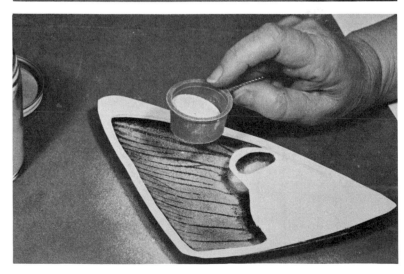

The lines can be left as they are or opaque enamel can be sifted very lightly over them for a more subtle effect.

Colors are walnut-brown transparent and ivory opaque with lighter siftings of pale yellow, chartreuse, and peach.

SGRAFFITO ENAMELS

Sgraffito is the process of scratching designs through an unfired layer of enamel to expose the surface underneath. This surface may be a fired base coat of enamel in a contrasting color or value, or it may be the bare copper surface. Sgraffito decoration appeals especially to craftsmen who like to sketch spontaneously. Scratched areas can vary from a hairline in width to much wider dimensions, depending on the scratching tool. Suitable tools may be anything with a point, either sharp or blunted. Toothpicks, a scriber, pencil, or the pointed wooden end of a small watercolor brush are objects that are readily available. Sgraffito is effective by itself; it may also be combined with other methods of surface enrichment. Its special advantage is that delicate or bold spontaneous linear patterns can be achieved with comparative ease.

To prepare an enameled or copper surface for a scratched sgraffito design, spray it with diluted gum or agar, then sift on a moderate layer of enamel. Spray it again *lightly*, and give it a second very light dusting of enamel with no final gum spraying. When the gum is dry, it is time for the actual scratching process. The design should be scribed freely and quickly so that lines are smooth and flowing. Then tip the piece so loosened enamel falls free onto a sheet of paper, where it may be retrieved for the enamel jar. Fire at 1450° F. until the enamel becomes shiny. When the piece has cooled, stone the edges carefully under running water and polish them with steel wool. Avoid striking the enamel with the abrasive stone, which would leave scratches. Steel wool will not scratch enamel.

First attempts may be very simple. Skill will soon develop, and more elaborate patterns can be attempted. Lines scratched

Footed bowl. Polly Rothenberg. Interior is transparent turquoise over turquoise opaque. Exterior, flux first, then a layer of royal-blue opaque fired. All firings at 1425° F. so the soldered rim foot will not melt loose.

through the unfired enamel while it is still slightly damp will form lines that are broad and feathery rather than those that are sharply defined. If the base surface is bare copper rather than fired enamel, the piece must be submerged in a pickling bath after it is fired, in order to remove firescale that has formed in the scratched-out areas. The solution must be weak so enameled areas are not injured. A solution of commercial Sparex or a weak solution of nitric acid, one part acid to six parts water, is suggested (remember, add acid to water, not water to acid). Leave the piece in the pickling solution for only a minute or two, rinse it, and polish it with steel wool. Repeat the process until the metal is clean. The surface may be left with the bare metal exposed or the entire surface can be covered with a transparent color before being given a final firing.

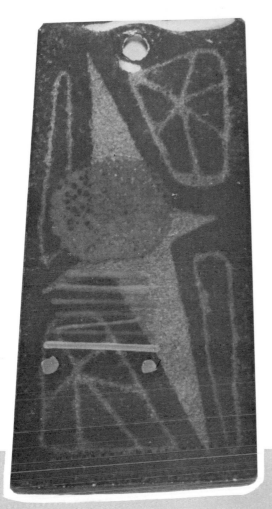

Pendant. William Gehl. Sgraffito and stencil. Courtesy of the American Art Clay Co.

Sgraffito trays. Courtesy of the American Art Clay Co.

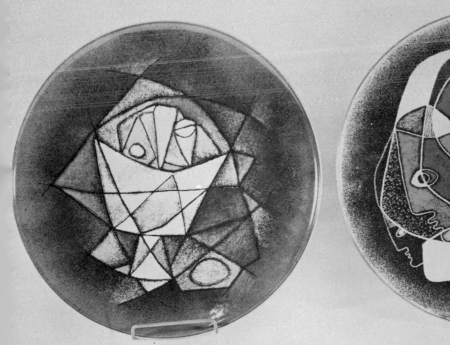
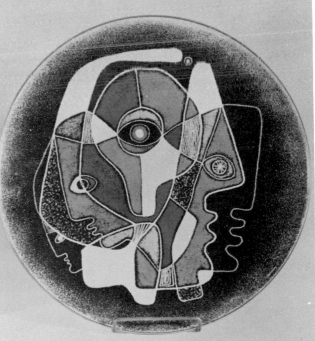

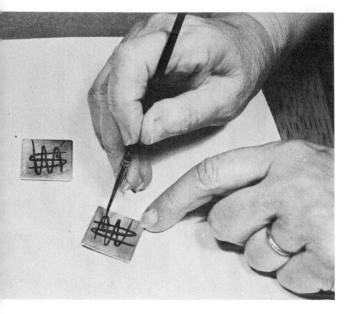

Underglaze is applied to the bare copper. Cuff-link designs should be reversed so they "face" each other.

The lines are dried, diluted gum is sprayed over the surface, and transparent enamel sifted over all. Because underglaze is an oil-base paint, the moist gum will not dissipate it.

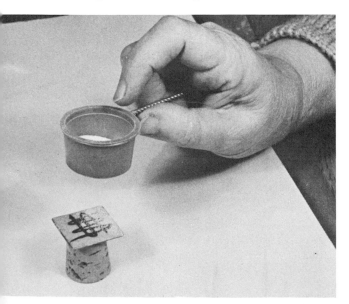

OVERGLAZE, UNDERGLAZE, AND METALLIC GLAZE

Fine Line Black and Jet Line Back are trade names for a dense black oil-base *overglaze* paint. It is valuable for applying fine black details with a pen or pointed brush to accent or finish a fired enamel surface. Stir the paint well before you use it. It tends to settle in the bottom of the bottle. If you use only the thin liquid at the top of the bottle, instead of stirring it, you will have a washed-out wispy line instead of a sharp black one.

Dip a small pointed brush or pen into the liquid and draw with it as you would with any paint. If it begins to build up on the brush, clean the brush from time to time with turpentine when you are doing extensive work on a piece. It will keep the lines clean and sharp.

Definitive overglaze lines can be combined with soft-edge stencils. Counterenamel the piece; then fire a base coat of a transparent or opaque color. Either the stencil patterns or the black overglaze lines can be applied first. Dry the overglaze on top of the hot kiln for about a half hour. Fire it quickly at 1450° F., just until the lines are shiny. Overfiring causes lines to fade, spread, and sink into the enamel.

Black *underglaze* must be stirred like overglaze because it also tends to settle when it has not been used for a while. Underglaze can be applied with pen or brush directly on clean bare copper. Cover it with transparent enamel, then fire it at 1400° F. It does not burn away. Underglaze can also be applied to a preenameled surface. It is covered with transparent enamel and fired in one firing. The black line design has the effect of being *in* the design rather than being applied on the surface. Overglaze and underglaze can be combined with metallic paints in the same composition.

Liquid gold and platinum metallic overglaze lusters are applied thinly on fired enameled-metal surfaces with brush or pen. They should not be applied too thinly or they will leave a watery purplish line instead of the desired metallic color. It is important to avoid getting finger smudges of luster on clean enameled surfaces. Even when you have wiped them off, some glaze remains and will make smudges when the piece is fired. If a line needs repairing, it is best to clean the entire surface with lighter fluid or carbon tetrachloride. For extra insurance, clean it two or three times.

Correct firing of metallic lusters is important. First the fumes must be driven off. Open the hot-kiln door and insert the piece (on a trivet) into the kiln; then immediately withdraw it. Do this two or three times; then sniff it. You will notice a strong pungent odor as the oils are driven off. The piece is put into the kiln and fired at 1400° F. The luster first will turn black, then bright gold or platinum. It must be left in the kiln *a little longer* to fuse the color completely. Count to ten, then quickly withdraw it. If a metallic design seems to burn away or become cracked, apply another coat of the liquid gold or platinum directly on the first coat, and refire it.

Underglaze painting. Karl Drerup. Colors were applied by wet inlay. Courtesy of the artist.

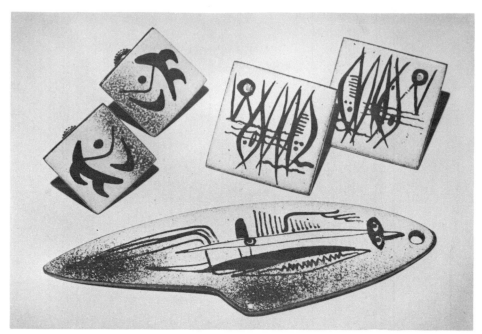

Earrings and pendant. Robert Engstrom. Opaque white enamel on copper has distinctive Jet Line Black overglaze designs. Courtesy of the artist.

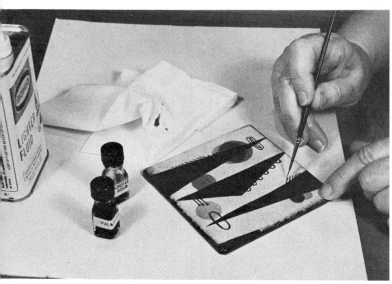

When liquid gold is fired, it appears light over dark enamel and dark over light colors. Tile edges have been bent down; corners are cut and shaped. Keep the brush tip clean so that lines will be sharp.

Simple stencil and gold drawings. Colors are brown, pink, and ivory.

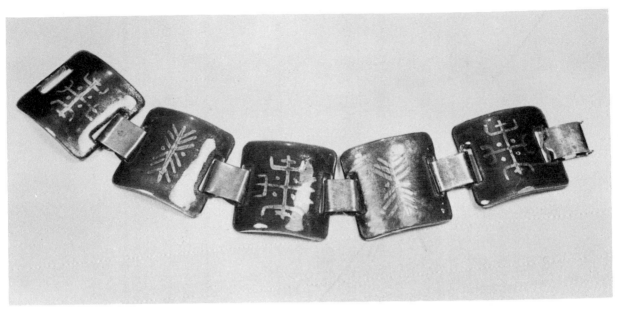

Hammered and shaped copper bracelet in 16-gauge, enameled in jungle-green transparent. Simple Indian designs are liquid gold.

Champlevé bowl. Noel Merrick. Liquid gold accents. Courtesy of American Art Clay Co.

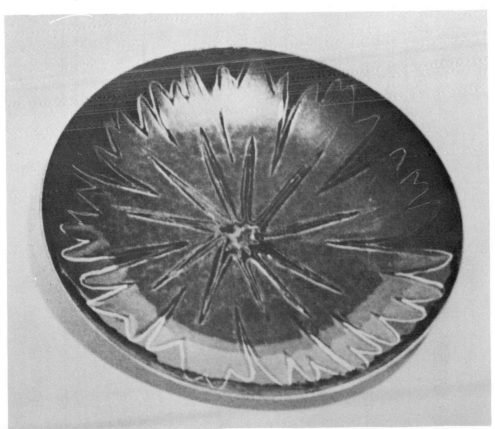

Overglaze panel. Mary Sharp. Piece was enameled on both sides. Sketch was
applied in overglaze with a pen. Courtesy of the artist.

Detail of APOSTLES panel.

APOSTLES. Mary Ellen McDermott. Panel in several techniques: stencil, dusting, wet inlay, overglaze, gold lines. Tiles are mounted on walnut panel, 40 inches by 16 inches. Courtesy of The Butler Institute of American Art, Youngstown, Ohio.

Simple Fine Line Black overglaze lines are applied over a fired flux base coat. Dry, and fire at 1400° F.

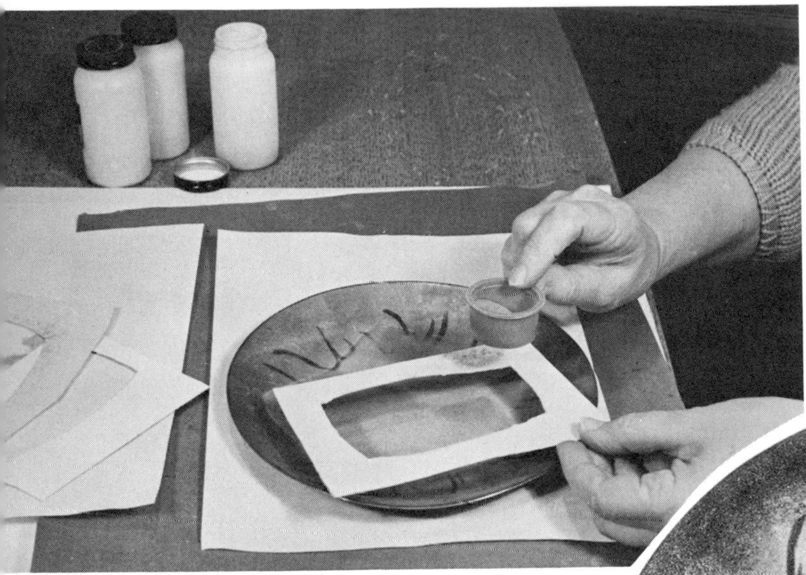

Three rectangular shapes are soft-stenciled in transparent red, green, and golden brown.

The finished tray has a fine sifting of opaque black around the border.

Soft stencil shapes with freely drawn fine black lines. Ferns are scrolled threads.

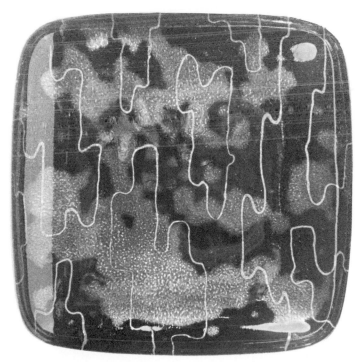

Square tray. Audrea Kreye. Flux designs were fired on bare copper. Transparent red was fired over all. The red appears light over the flux designs. Gold luster lines were drawn in free-form linear pattern. Courtesy of the artist.

Threads of varying thickness make a more interesting design.

A preformed convex disk is enameled on both sides. Red and black opaque are dusted over the gray base coat. Threads are dipped into gum and positioned according to a sketch. Fire at 1400° F.

ENAMEL THREADS AND LUMPS

Lengths of brightly colored opaque enamel threads, with their endless variety of curves and twisted loops, form intriguing design patterns. Threads can be combined with other forms of decoration, such as stencil, luster, and overglaze. When used in combination with other methods of decoration, they should be applied just before the final firing because each ensuing firing softens the sharp, clean lines of the threads. They are especially effective in creating whimsical animal, bird, and insect designs. Threads and lumps also lend themselves readily to nonrepresentational patterns.

Some interesting effects can be made by firing threads directly on clean bare copper.

The resultant firescale around the threads can be incorporated into a design; or the piece can be put into a pickling solution, cleaned, dried, and briskly polished. Dip the threads into full-strength enameling gum, and position them on the bare copper. Let the gum dry completely. It is best to use 16-gauge copper, and then omit any counter-enamel. The counterenamel would warp the metal because the threads would not supply enough countertension on the surface of the piece. Fire the threads on bare copper at 1450° F.

Any piece made of sheet metal must be counterenameled when the top surface will have *enamel lumps* applied to it; otherwise the lumps may fracture or even pop loose some time after the piece has cooled. This caution does not apply to sturdy cast metal. Because silver castings have dramatic form,

enamels are most frequently applied to them in small amounts for bright accents. Tiny transparent lumps are like small gems when they are fired on silver jewelry.

Some opaque lumps are high-firing. They require temperatures above 1500° F. for best results. These colors are beige, yellow, ivory, and hard white. It is well to take this into consideration when combining them with other lump colors. Soft-fusing lumps that melt at 1300° F. are best for scrolled patterns because they become liquid when fired at 1400° F. Scrolled enamels are discussed on a later page.

Transparent enamel lumps show the true beauty of colors when they are fired over a flux base. Dip the lumps into undiluted gum, and position them. When the gum has dried, fire them until they melt and sink into pools of brilliant color.

TIMID LION. Enameled on a precoated steel tile. Body section is sharp stencil. Ruff and head area is formed by holding a cardboard disk above the surface for a soft-edge stencil. Colors are brown, orange, and turquoise. Threads are black.

Whimsical pendants. Gerri Nichols. Preformed pendant shapes with lump and thread patterns.

KABUKI DANCER. Gerri Nichols. Costume is stenciled. Mrs. Nichols designs directly with the threads, and lets their curves dictate the character of the figures. Courtesy of the artist.

Free-form tray. Lillian Skaggs. Lumps of transparent turquoise and green-gold were fired over a net stencil. Courtesy of the artist.

Hand-raised bowl. Lillian Skaggs. This graceful piece was formed of 14-gauge copper, by using mallets, hammers, and anvils. The inside of the bowl is enameled in opaque robin's-egg blue, fired, then three coats of transparent turquoise applied and fired. Chartreuse opaque was next sifted over a net stencil. Transparent lumps were positioned and fired flat. Transparent brown counterenamel. Courtesy of the artist.

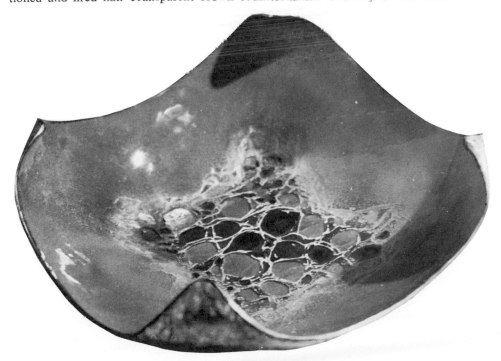

Silver pin. Audrey Engstrom. Formed sterling silver "pod" with inner element of cast pure silver. Blue, purple, and red transparent enamel jewel tips. Courtesy of the artist. *Photo by Robert Engstrom.*

CHILDREN PLAYING. White enamel threads were dipped in gum and applied to 16-gauge copper panel, directly on the bare metal.

CRACKLE ENAMELS

An exciting characteristic of crackle enamels is the variety of attractive patterns they create when they are fired over a pre-fired undercoat of enamel. Certain factors influence the manner in which this enamel will check or craze: the thickness of the undercoat, the thickness of the crackle-enamel application, temperatures at which they are fired, the length of firing time, and the fusing characteristics of individual colors. Variations in the crackle patterns can be developed from experimentation with these factors. When a piece is fired at 1450° F., a network of cracks appears in the enamel; the longer the piece is in the kiln, the wider the cracks become. Interesting speckled areas develop where the enamel is applied in a thin layer. If the crackle enamel is applied over a fired undercoat of a *transparent* enamel, cracks will develop more fully than over a base coat of opaque enamel. Although they will checker somewhat on flat pieces, they perform most effectively on those with sloping sides. Crackle enamels are primarily intended for decorative use. They do not readily fuse to bare metal.

These special enamels can be purchased in either liquid or dry form. The liquid variety should never be allowed to dry out and become caked, because it is almost impossible to restore it to a usable condition by adding water, no matter how diligently one tries to blend it. Fresh, properly prepared liquid crackle has a creamy consistency right up to the top of the jar. It is wise to buy it in amounts that will be used up rather soon. If a few drops of water are added to it before it is put away, it will have less tendency to dry out.

The dry powdered form is made liquid by the addition of water. Crackle enamel is always applied to a shape in liquid form. Stir the dry enamel into water until it has the consistency of thick cream. Blend it until all lumps disappear.

A soft watercolor brush is best for ap-

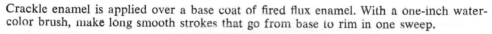

Crackle enamel is applied over a base coat of fired flux enamel. With a one-inch water-color brush, make long smooth strokes that go from base to rim in one sweep.

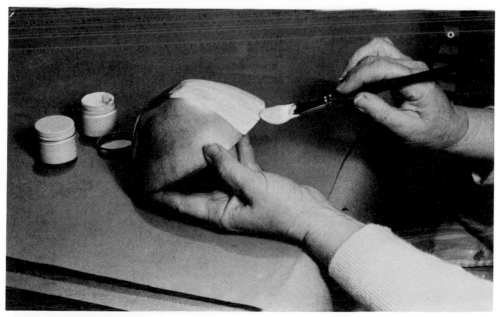

plying this enamel. Avoid going over a stroke the second time, once it has been applied. For interesting variations, some thick and some thin strokes might be applied to the same piece. Make long smooth strokes that go quickly, rather than strokes brushed in short circles. The brush should be full of enamel, but not dripping. When the side of a bowl is completely covered, the base can be given a few short circular strokes. Let the piece dry completely.

A design can be added with a pointed scriber, much in a manner similar to sgraf-fito, except that the line is more like a cut than like a visible line. During the firing process, the enamel will separate along these cuts as well as in a natural crackle pattern.

This special kind of enamel makes a strong texture that combines well with plain areas. A beautiful effect is achieved with a base coat of flux enamel. The flux fires to a golden color that appears like a network of gold lines through the covering crackle color. It is especially effective when the covering coat of crackle is a dark color or black.

A pattern may be cut into the dried enamel. The cutting tool should be sharp, and strokes should be free and sketchy.

When the piece is fired, enamel separates along the cuts, as well as in a natural crackled pattern.

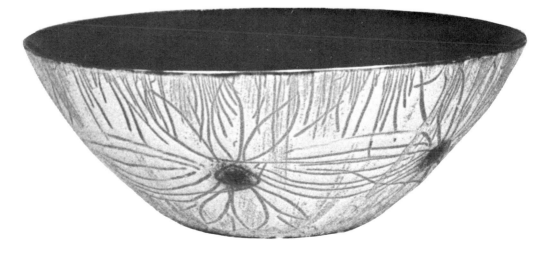

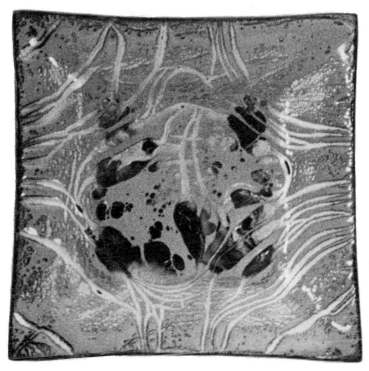

Soft-fusing transparent lumps of enamel were fired into the
base coat of flux before turquoise crackle was applied. A
few loose curved strokes were cut into the dry crackle before
it was fired. Collection of Mr. and Mrs. Herbert Tepping.

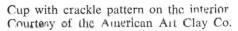

Cup with crackle pattern on the interior.
Courtesy of the American Art Clay Co.

SILVER AND GOLD FOILS, GOLD LEAF

Silver Foil

When silver foil is applied to an enameled surface, then fired and covered with a layer of fired transparent enamel, it gives a sparkling, jewel-like quality that is valuable for accenting and enriching certain areas of a design.

Some differences will occur in the appearance of the foil, depending on the type of enamel used for a base-coat and whether the surface is flat or inclined. On a hard or high-firing enamel, and on flat surfaces, there is less movement of the molten enamel during firing, and consequently less movement and

crinkling of the foil. It will be smoother and less likely to split after repeated firings. On an inclined surface or over a low-fusing enamel, as the piece fires, there is more tendency for the enamel to flow and crinkle the foil further. This can be an advantage when it is covered by the wet-inlay method. The resultant increase in refraction of light rays from the crinkled foil and the thickness of wet-packed washed transparent enamel create an embedded-jewel effect that is rich but not garish.

Foil must be cut between layers of tracing paper because it is too fragile to be cut with bare scissors. It must be pierced with a needle to allow gases and moisture to escape when it is fired to enamel.

Foil shapes are cut out between layers of tracing paper. Bare fingers would possibly tear or soil it.

The foil must be pierced all over to allow steam and gases to escape when it is fired. A needle anchored in a cork is a good tool for this process.

Spray or brush gum over the enameled surface; then press a damp brush lightly on the foil shape, pick it up, and position it on the enamel. When all foil pieces have dried, fire at 1450° F. until they are red-hot and flat.

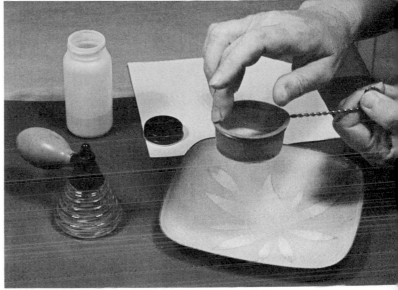

When the foil has been fired and cooled, spray it with gum solution and sift transparent enamel over it. Fire at 1450° F. Additional colors can be trailed, sifted, or wet-packed.

Overglaze lines and gold luster are applied and fired.

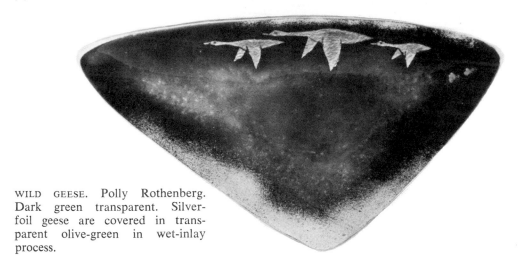

WILD GEESE. Polly Rothenberg. Dark green transparent. Silver-foil geese are covered in transparent olive-green in wet-inlay process.

A full-scale design for gold foil and gold leaf is drawn in color.

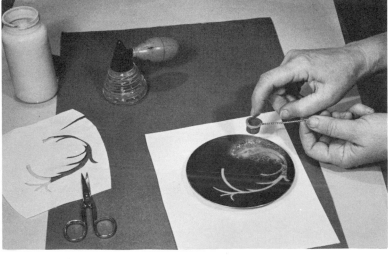

The stem is traced onto paper toweling and cut out for a stencil. It is moistened and positioned on a tray that has been enameled and counterenameled. With a ½-inch sifter, a light opaque enamel is dusted around the stencil.

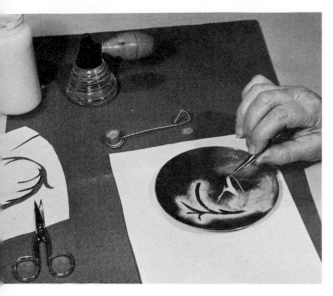

The stencil is removed with tweezers. When it is dry, the tray is fired at 1450° F.

Gold-foil areas are traced and cut out between leaves of tracing paper.

Gold Foil

Gold foil is tissue-thin pure gold. Like silver foil, it fuses perfectly to a preenameled surface when it is fired at regular enameling temperatures. Gold foil is thinner than silver foil, and is more difficult to handle. It is best to start with very small pieces until you have achieved some dexterity in handling them. The warm colors, especially transparent red, are quite handsome fired over gold.

Gold Leaf

Leaf in 23-karat gold is available as a thin film of gold dust adhered to a tissue-paper backing sheet. In this method, the gold is *not removed* from the backing sheet before its application to an *enameled* surface. Like foils, these gold-covered sheets are sold interleaved in small books of thin paper. They can usually be bought in art supply stores.

Draw a design on folded tracing paper and place one of the gold-covered tissue sheets between the folded leaves of paper. (Remember, the leaf is not removed from its

Foil shapes are carefully pierced with a sharp needle. Gold foil is easily torn.

If the foil tends to wrap around the brush, it may be wise to use smaller pieces. Gold-foil shapes are transferred to the tray with a soft brush.

When the tray is dry, it is positioned securely on a trivet and lifted into the kiln. It is fired at 1450° F. until all pieces are flat.

Washed transparent 80-mesh enamel colors are put into separate containers. A few drops of gum are added to each color, and blended. With a tiny wet-inlay spatula, pick up colors and pack them over each foil shape. A small brush or pointed tool can be used to help guide colors into place.

backing sheet.) When the designs have been cut out, place them on the table while gum is brushed over the enameled surface that will receive the gold leaf. Each piece must be positioned on the exact spot where it will remain because it cannot be moved around like gold foil; gold leaf will quickly cling to the damp enameled surface. Its tissue backing sheet will soak up some of the gum moisture.

Carefully press a small wad of facial tissue against the back of each piece to remove excess moisture and assure good adhesion between the gold leaf and the enameled surface. Let it dry a few moments before you remove the backing sheet. It will loosen as the piece dries, and can be picked off with tweezers.

The firing temperature for leaf is very critical. If it is overfired, it will burn away and vanish. When the piece is dry, fire it at 1350° F. until it is cherry-red, not a bright orange heat.

Gold leaf can be left bare or it may be covered with low-fusing flux. It will form a delicate weblike gold pattern if a coat of flux is fired over it. It must be applied in a thin dusting; wet inlay would be too thick. The firing temperature must be kept at 1350° F. The higher the temperature, the more the gold will disintegrate. Remove it from the kiln the moment the flux turns shiny. Gold leaf should be applied as the final touch to a completed design because subsequent firings will completely destroy it.

Moisture is drawn off with a tissue. The tray is dried and fired at 1450° F.

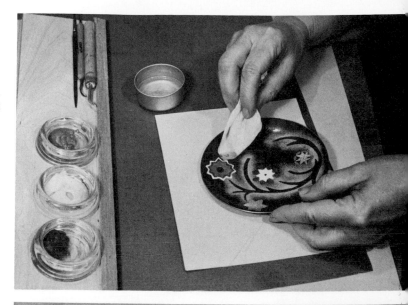

Gold-leaf shapes are cut out through all three leaves of paper. The gold has not been removed from its backing sheet.

Notice that each gold-leaf shape is positioned in the exact spot where it will remain. To move it around would drag the gold off its backing sheet.

After the tray has been fired and cooled, soft-fusing flux is sifted over each fired leaf shape.

The gold leaf has formed a delicate web pattern.

A base coat of dark-gray transparent enamel was fired on both sides of a large tray. Torn-out paper stencils are arranged on the surface and diluted gum is sprayed over them. Opaque enamels in colors of dark red, blue, green, orange, and some purple are sifted around the stencil edges. For good control, a very small sifter is essential.

STENCIL, SILVER FOIL, AND TEXTURE

Stencil enamels can be combined creatively with other methods of surface enrichment. When design areas are laid out with stencils, they can be covered or combined with wet inlay and silver or gold foils. Highfiring enamels can also be applied in selected areas to create texture; they are trailed by hand or applied over a second set of stencils. These high-firing enamels, both in transparent and opaque, are available in a coarser grind than the more common 80-mesh, and are sometimes called granular glass lumps. They may vary from 10- to 20-mesh, but they can be ground under water to a finer size with an agate mortar and pestle. Because of the extreme hardness of this enamel, a mortar and pestle of softer composition would become scarred and nicked during the grinding operation. The water will prevent pieces of the enamel flying into the room while it is being ground. Enamel should be washed after grinding, to clean it of all "fines" or powdered enamel that might cause cloudiness in the fired design.

Scoop the ground-washed enamel onto a piece of heavy aluminum foil and dry it in a warm oven or on top of the hot kiln. The dry enamel is sifted, first with a 200-mesh sifter to separate the finest particles, then with an 80-mesh sifter, and finally with a sifter of 60-mesh. The remaining granules can be reground. The various mesh sizes are stored in separate containers, for possible future use.

When this coarse hard enamel is applied to a design, it is fired at the same temperature as medium-fusing enamel. The particles will become rounded, but they will form a textured surface instead of sinking into the background color. If an 80-mesh, medium-fusing, lighter opaque color is fired first, and the harder enamel is sifted and fired over it, the light color will set off and dramatize the granular texture of the hard enamel. Exciting designs can be formed by stenciling a dark, hard-texture enamel over a lighter background of the *same color,* such as dark-blue transparent hard granular enamel over an opaque medium-blue background. Fire both enamels at 1450° F.

Stencils are removed with tweezers. The piece is dried and fired at 1450° F. Between firings, the tray edge is rubbed with steel wool to prevent firescale buildup.

Silver foil paillons are prepared as described under "Silver Foil." When the foil has been applied, it is fired and cooled.

Each foil paillon is packed with moist transparent enamels. If the enamel seems to dry out during wet application, it should be sprayed lightly to keep it moist. When the enamel is packed and dry, it is fired at 1450° F.

Hard black enamels in coarse mesh size are ground in water to prevent pieces of enamel from flying into the room. They are dried and sifted to size.

A second set of stencils is positioned over the foil areas. Medium-gray opaque is sifted around stencil edges; then the hard black enamel is sifted over the gray enamel through a 60-mesh strainer. Stencils are removed. The lighter enamel will sink beneath the harder black enamel that fuses but does not flatten at 1500° F. It dramatizes the crusty texture of the hard black enamel.

Before firing the piece, pick up all gray and black enamel with a brush from areas where it has strayed so the texturing is confined to planned areas. The piece is dried and fired at 1500° F. Black line accents may be added and a final firing given at 1400° F.

The completed tray.

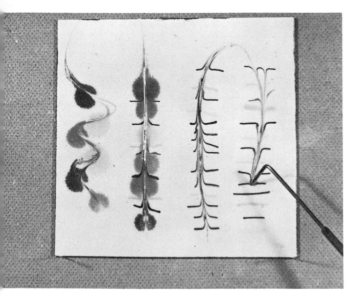

Initial attempts at scrolling are made on a practice tile. The tool should glide easily through molten enamel.

The tray is anchored securely on a winged trivet. Here the door is opened to show the tool poised for scrolling, but it should be opened only about half as wide when actual swirling is done.

SCROLLED ENAMELS

Delicately scrolled enamel designs are created in the kiln when red-hot enamel threads and low-firing lumps are swirled over an enamel base coat with a special scrolling tool. The best results are obtained when there is at least one coat of transparent enamel on the surface of the copper shape. Transparent enamels have lower melting temperatures than opaques, and are not so quick to stiffen suddenly during the scrolling process. If you prefer an opaque background, first fire a *flux* base coat to the copper surface, then add a thin layer of the opaque color enamel, and fire it. It is best to fire the background enamels before adding threads or lumps for swirling just to be sure that edges are adequately covered. It is too late to repair thin or pitted edges after a design has been swirled. A delicate scrolled pattern will deteriorate with each succeding firing.

The type of lumps that give the most successful results are low-firing transparent lumps and small flat opaque lumps; they should melt perfectly flat without the base coat of enamel becoming overfired. Large opaque lumps are not very successful for scrolling. Beige, yellow, ivory, and hard white opaque lumps are the last to melt and the first to stiffen during the scrolling process. It is apparent that the selection of materials and the preparation of the piece are most important for success in scrolling enamels.

If any design that uses lumps is to remain in good condition, and not crack and chip loose sometime after it is fired, the copper shape must first be counterenameled. This seems to rule out scrolling in a small tabletop jewelry kiln; however, many attractive designs, consisting of swirled threads only, remain intact on a piece that is not counterenameled, if the surface is slightly convex.

Carefully controlled scrolling. Threads were laid diagonally. The pendant was swirled in a jewelry kiln, then it was counterenameled in a large kiln.

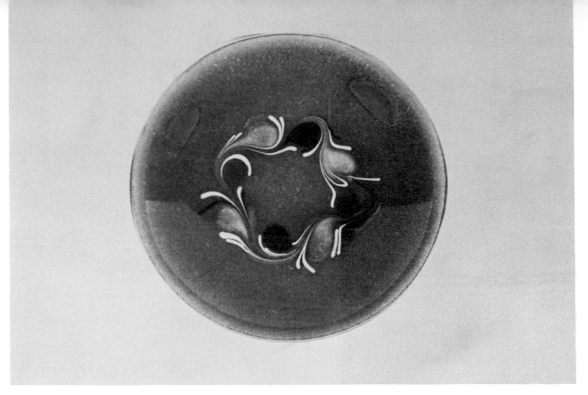

Scrolled tray. Audrea Kreye. Background is gray-blue transparent. Threads were laid between lumps for scrolling. Courtesy of the artist.

Deep bowl. Stencil combined with very small lumps and scrolled threads.

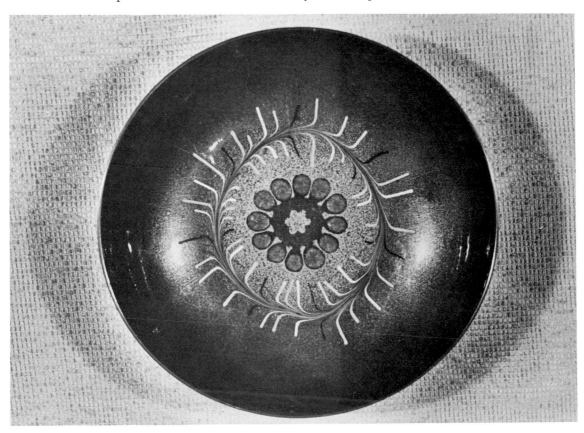

Top left: Repoussé bowl. Enameled in transparent colors. Polly Rothenberg.

Top right: Chinaman and Rice Bowl. Enamel portrait. Hamilton Aaris.

Center left: Cloisonné bowl lid. Mary Sharp.

Center right: Two. Sculptural shapes mounted on walnut. Polly Rothenberg.

Bottom right: Enamel painting. Karl Drerup.

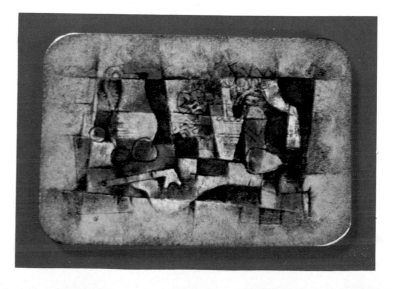

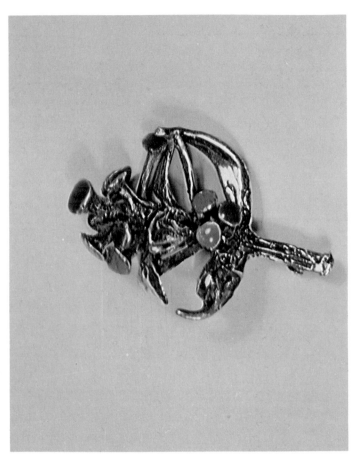

Cast gold pin with green
enamel jewels. Audrey
Engstrom.

Bouquet. Enameled cast silver pin.
Ruth Tepping.

Box lid panels. Textured enamels
from treated copper and additives.
Catherine Munter.

Color schemes and designs should be worked out carefully in advance. When the work is under way, a feeling of confidence will result in a more smoothly executed project. It will have more rhythmic vitality. There is an old Chinese painter's saying: "In planning be careful and deliberate, but when the brush is in hand show courage and self-confidence." When the scrolling tool is in hand, to hesitate part way through the design for lack of planning may well ruin it. Because the materials are so decorative in themselves, there may be a temptation to melt some lumps and threads and just "stir them around." The result may be eye-catching, but it does not begin to exploit the real design potential of scrolling. It is well to sketch the "route" to be followed by the scrolling tool, preferably on a piece of cardboard, and place it near the kiln for easy reference. A simple design can be executed freely and rapidly. A light touch will prevent the tool from bearing down against the copper and exposing it. Take a few practice swings in the air with the tool before the kiln door is opened.

The scrolling tool should be a long one equipped with a heat shield. Sometimes beginners will attempt to scroll a pattern with a short, shieldless tool and without wearing a protective mitt. Their hands become scorched, and they are prejudiced against scrolling before they have begun to create any designs.

The kiln must be really hot and enamels must get red-hot and *as soft as melted butter* before the tool touches them. There should be no feeling of resistance against the tool as it glides through the hot enamel. If the enamel begins to get tacky during the swirling, it is imperative to withdraw the tool immediately, close the kiln door, and allow the piece to become red-hot again. When the process is resumed, start behind the interrupted point and draw the tool through the spot to smooth it out again. This may not be easy for the beginner. How-

ever, by starting with straight strokes on a practice tile, you will gain confidence with each succeeding attempt.

Sometimes withdrawing a tool can be a problem. A thread of cooling enamel clings to the tool and pulls an endless enamel string with it. The easiest solution is to draw the tool off the edge of the piece at some logical design point, instead of lifting it off. Sometimes a slight snap of the wrist may release the tool from the enamel. However, if the enamel has become cool and thickened, remove the trivet and the tool from the kiln and tap the tool loose from the enamel where it has become mired. It is much wiser to remove the tool from the kiln at the first sign of thickening in the enamel, and avoid this problem altogether.

The prepared copper piece on which the scrolling will be done must be securely anchored on a sturdy trivet. The piece must be held *firmly* between the wings or prongs of metal that extend above it. The trivet is very important. If it is too lightweight, the scrolling process may drag it around. Stilts will not work!

While the piece is heating, the path the tool will take can be checked with the sketch that has been placed nearby; it can be practiced a few times in the air. In three to four minutes, the piece will be red-hot. With hand protected by an asbestos mitt, hold the door open far enough to admit the tool and allow for free movement. Trace your strokes lightly and quickly through the melted lumps; then withdraw the tool and close the door for a few seconds to allow the enamel to flatten out where it has been swirled. Remove the piece from the kiln, let it cool, then stone and polish the edges.

When you have tried the swirling process a few times, you may want to attempt more intricate designs. If scrolling is considered as a decorative device rather than an end in itself, many beautiful designs can be created by combining it with other methods of surface enrichment.

ART GLASS APPLIED TO ENAMEL AND COPPER

Cathedral art glass fuses at temperatures consistent with that of enamels. Colors are attractive and predictable. This art glass is available in small 8-inch by 10-inch sheets, ⅛ inch thick. Some stained glass has one or more colors applied to both sides, but it is not colored all the way through. This type of glass is not suitable for our purpose. Bits of scrap glass, so useful to glass craftsmen, are not recommended for application to enamels. If they are soft-fusing, they tend to ball up and lose shape. If the glass is very hard, it will not fuse before the enamels are overfired.

After planning your design, you will need to be able to cut glass. A carbide wheel glass cutter is the best tool for this process. Place the sheet of glass, smooth side up, on a resilient surface such as a flat-napped carpet remnant or a magazine. It is easiest to try small squares and rectangles first. Lay a straightedge on the glass and score along it until you get the feel of the cutter. The first cut might be along one end of the sheet of glass. Hold the cutter near perpendicular with one hand. With the other hand exerting even pressure on the glass, draw the cutter firmly in one continuous sweep from one end of the glass to the other. Avoid going over it a second time. Pick up the sheet of glass and *turn it over*. Tap smartly along the line you have just scored, using the metal ball end of the glass cutter. If you have made a firm continuous scored line on the reverse side, the glass should fall apart. Some practice may be necessary before you succeed. You should now have a long, slender strip of glass that may be cut crosswise in the same manner, making little squares and rectangles. When you cut shapes that are not rectangular or square, cut short straight lines from edge to edge of the glass and fol-

low the contours of the shape you want to cut out. Then file or sand the corners away until you have the desired shape. Take care to prevent glass chips from flying into your eyes. Filing can be done under water. Glass craftsmen use large shapes that require intricate cutting ability, but the enamelist uses small, simple shapes for bright accents. Pieces of glass should be fired and edges rounded before they are applied to an enameled or bare copper surface.

The temperatures at which glass is fired control the effects we seek. At 1350° F. the glass will fuse to enamel but will retain edges that are too sharp. At 1400° F. the edges become blunted, though still retaining shape. As the temperature rises, the edges become more rounded, and as it continues toward 1500° F. a rectangular shape becomes an oval or cabochon. Above 1500° F. the glass loses some of its form and becomes a molten mass, with some of its color impaired. An angular glass shape will retain its form if the firing temperature is held between 1400° F. and 1450° F., when *cathedral glass* is used. That is the difference between using glass and using lump enamel. Enamel lumps will form balls as firing continues. The embedded glass is not likely to fracture when it is removed from the kiln (if it has been counterenameled), because the red-hot metal allows it to cool slowly. Avoid fast-cooling it under water or with a fan.

Glass shapes for use on enamels are usually prefired at 1400° F. When they have been removed from the kiln and cooled, they are separated from the mica with a stiff brush. If mica adheres to glass, nothing will fuse to it. This is often a cause for failure when glass is tried by enamelers.

A fairly thick layer of counterenamel must be fired to the clean surface directly back of areas where glass shapes will be fused; this will equalize tensions on both sides. If this is neglected, shortly after the

The end of the carbide glass cutter has notches that can be used to break off small pieces of glass.

Notice that the cutter is held with the flat part between thumb and forefinger.

glass bits are fired, and as they cool, faint cracking sounds will warn us that very soon some glass fragments may fracture loose. When a metal piece is fired, it becomes quite malleable. As the metal cools, it flexes; but glass does not flex, of course. If the metal shape is *not* counterenameled first, as soon as it is removed from the kiln the glass will fracture when the cooling metal flexes and warps away from the glass piece. Even after metal has cooled, changes in room temperature can cause it to flex. Counterenamel holds the metal firm and prevents this flexing action.

Another important requirement is to fire the enameled surface *before* you apply glass shapes; this assures two similar densities fusing together. If glass is placed on unfired enamel for fusing, countless tiny air pockets in the powdered enamel become trapped beneath the dense glass. In order to fire these unequal densities long enough to fuse them sufficiently, the design may become over-fired.

When glass pieces have been shaped and the surface has been prepared, dip each glass piece into undiluted gum and position it into place. When the gum is dry, sift soft-fusing flux over the glass shapes, then brush it off the top of each shape so the piece of glass is surrounded by a "collar" of unfired flux. This flux collar will melt and give the glass shapes an embedded quality. Fire at 1450° F. until the flux is shiny.

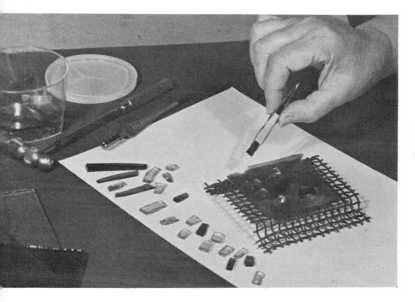

Small pieces of glass are spread on a sheet of mica that is placed on a trivet for firing.

Test panels for cathedral glass (other glass may fire differently). Left to right: unfired pieces; pieces fired to 1400° F.; pieces fired to 1450° F.; pieces fired to 1500° F.

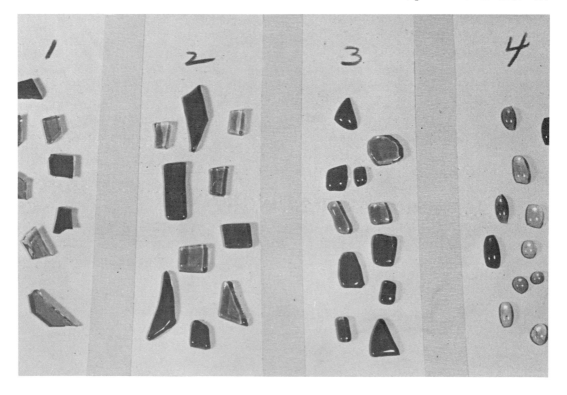

When the rounded shapes have been dipped into full-strength gum, they are positioned and dried. Soft-fusing flux is dusted over them. It is brushed off the tops so it falls in little "collars" of flux around each glass piece.

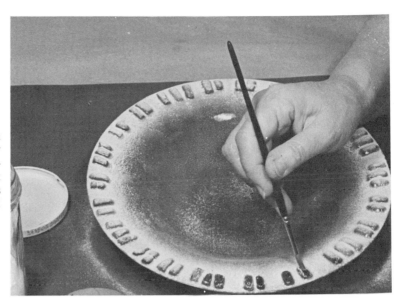

Glass colors are deep purple, turquoise, and green.

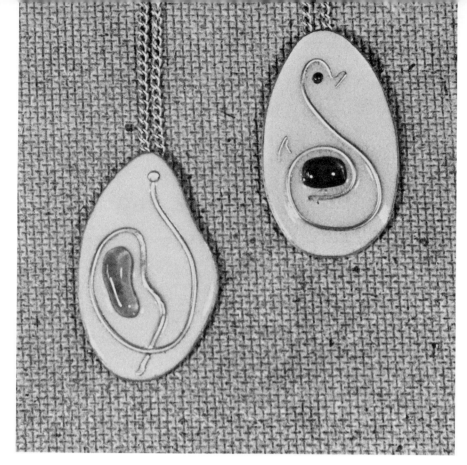

White opaque pendants with embedded wire and bright cathedral glass.

Glass Fused to Bare Copper
(Wind Chimes Project)

A bare copper surface that will receive a piece of fused glass must first be counter-enameled if the glass is to remain firmly attached to the metal, because of the flexing action of metal. Otherwise the glass will very likely pop loose as soon as it is removed from the kiln.

There is a second hazard encountered in firing glass on bare copper. When the small glass shape has been fired on mica in preparation for application to a surface, it will not fit perfectly flush with the metal. This is caused by variations in the mica that leave indented places in the fired glass. If the glass does not fit snugly to the copper, it will be found during firing that oxidation takes place where tiny air spaces occur. Resultant firescale will prevent the glass from fusing to the metal. This condition does not affect glass fired to an enamel surface.

To solve this problem, spread a *thin* layer of moist, low-fusing flux enamel to the undersurface of the glass shape; then press it firmly against the copper to exclude air. When the enamel has dried, the piece is fired at 1400° F. long enough for the flux to melt and the glass to fuse to the copper. This should take at least three minutes or longer. When the flux appears shiny around the edges of the glass shape, the trivet is removed from the kiln and allowed to cool slowly. When cool, the piece is put into warm pickling solution (not cold) in order to remove firescale from the copper. Metal edges are stoned and rubbed with steel wool.

Chime shapes and a spiral support section are cut from 18-gauge copper. Holes are drilled along the lower edge of the support before it is bent.

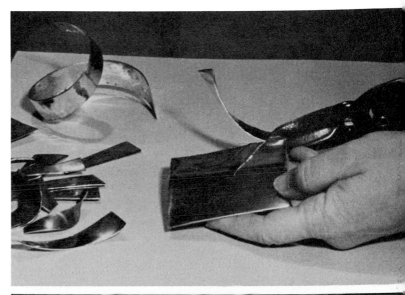

Copper pieces are flattened with a leather mallet so glass shapes will fit flush on the metal.

Suspension support is pounded all over to give it texture and strength. A piece of laminated plastic cabinet top makes a fine pounding surface.

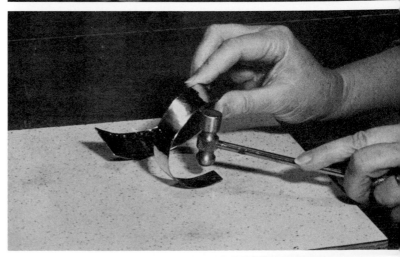

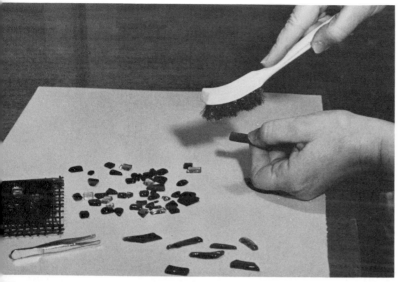

Glass pieces are fired on mica. All mica is removed with a brass brush.

Moistened flux is added to the back of each fired glass piece before it is placed against the bare metal for firing. *Metal pieces are counter-enameled.*

Pieces are ready for assembling. Those in the lower row have glass fused to bare copper. Those in the top row have long glass shards fused to an enameled surface. All pieces are counterenameled.

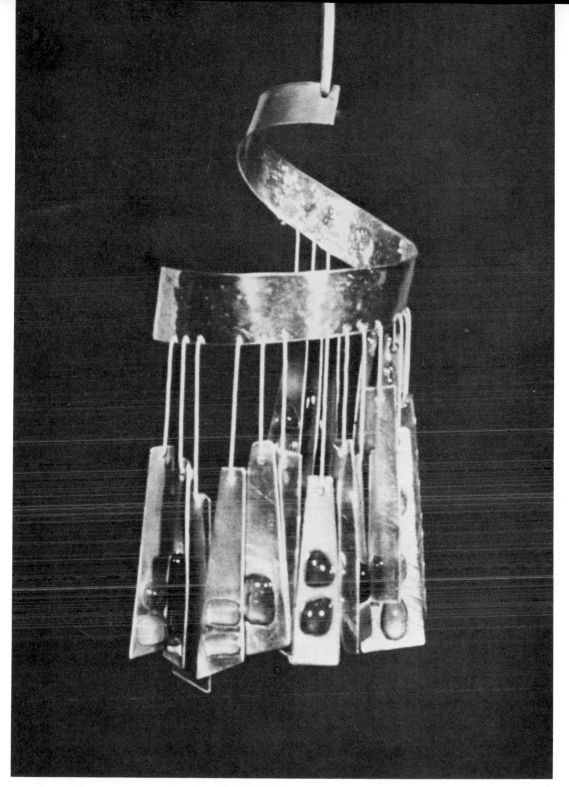

The chimes are suspended with knotted fishline cords. The mobile support is suspended by one thong.

CRUSHED GLASS FUSED TO ENAMELED COPPER

When crushed glass is applied to enameled copper, glass particles must be quite small and of fairly uniform size in order to fuse securely. For the most successful results, glass should fuse at temperatures compatible with the fusing temperature of enamel. Cathedral glass (commercial stained glass) fuses to enamel and also takes on slightly rounded form at 1450° F. It will fuse at lower temperatures, but it may retain sharp, jagged corners.

A slightly convex shape is not likely to flex while it cools and thus fracture glass applied to it. When the planned piece has been cut, smoothed, shaped, and scoured clean of all grease and soil, a medium-thick coat of sifted enamel is fired to the underneath side for counterenamel. This layer of enamel will hold the metal firm while crushed glass is fired to the top. When a suitable enamel color has also been applied to the top surface, and then fired, it is time to prepare the glass.

Glass should be crushed against a firm surface. A section of laminated plastic cabinet top, such as Formica, makes an excellent board on which to crush glass. Cabinet-top remnants are available at most cabinet shops. Lay some glass *between* folds of heavy canvas and pound it well with a sturdy hammer. Hands and eyes must be protected from the sharp glass. *Never scoop up crushed glass with bare hands!*

Put some of the crushed glass into a small shallow container. The larger pieces should be picked out with tweezers so that only small particles are used. Blend full-strength liquid gum or agar with the crushed glass. This mixture can be spooned onto an enameled surface such as a pendant, panel, or the flange of a tray. Pack it firmly with a tiny spatula. The next important step is to sift some soft-fusing flux over it. Flux will speed the fusing process and bind the glass particles together when they are fired. After a final spraying with diluted gum, the piece is dried and fired at 1450° F. until the flux appears shiny and the glass particles are fused and rounded. If any glass protrudes slightly over the edge of the enameled shape, take care that it is not broken off when the edge is rubbed with steel wool to smooth it after it has cooled. The glass will remain firmly attached and not crack loose if all steps are followed in detail.

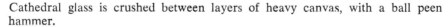

Cathedral glass is crushed between layers of heavy canvas, with a ball peen hammer.

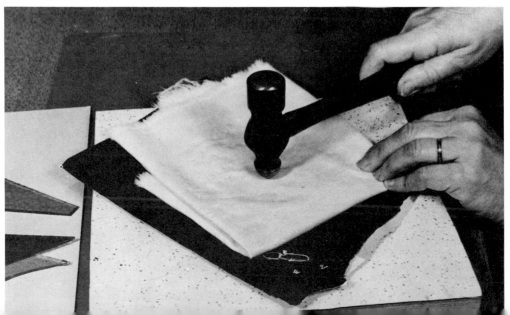

A shaped pendant form is cut from 18-gauge copper. It is made convex by being pounded over a slightly curved steel stake with a leather mallet. After it is cleaned, it is enameled on both sides with flux.

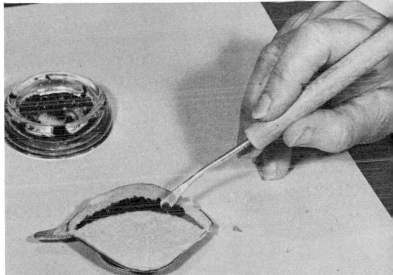

Crushed sapphire-blue cathedral glass is mixed with undiluted gum, and distributed over a stencil opening with a very small spatula.

Crushed light-turquoise glass is filled in the rest of the surface, and one rounded glass piece is positioned. Soft-fusing flux is sifted over all. The flux binds the glass and aids in its fusing.

Pendant's loop is curled back with round-nosed jewelry pliers.

A round convex two-inch disk was the base for crushed glass, silver foil, and black overglaze lines.

EMBEDDED WIRE DESIGNS

Copper, silver, or gold wire designs can be successfully embedded in an enameled surface. It is advisable to experiment with a spare length of the less expensive copper wire until you have achieved some facility in handling it. Wire can be bent and manipulated into broad curves with the fingers. For sharper curves you should use small jewelry pliers whose jaws are protected with tape to prevent deep scratches in the wire. If your first efforts seem kinky and mangled, they can be put aside in a scrap box and a fresh start made with smooth pieces. When wire has been "worked" for a while, it becomes stiff and brittle. It must be *annealed* in the same manner as sheet metal. It can be polished with steel wool to remove firescale. Then it can be smoothed and reused.

To smooth the wire, draw it tightly back and forth at right angles across the edge of a table or cabinet; then cut it into shorter usable lengths. The pieces should be handled carefully so they stay smooth. Wire designs should have clean sweeping lines and not be full of unplanned kinks and squiggles. When you have worked with a piece of scrap wire and have learned its qualities, limitations, and potentials, you should be ready to use either gold, silver, or copper wire with confidence. By bending the wire and working with it, you will discover better patterns than by forcing it into realistic shapes.

There are a number of ways to add variation and texture to embedded wire designs. Wire can be pounded, to add interest. The texture resulting from hammer blows is quite decorative. Small dots punched from scrap copper with a metal punch can add further variety. Wire shapes are essentially

Cut a pendant shape from cardboard and score around it on 18-gauge copper.

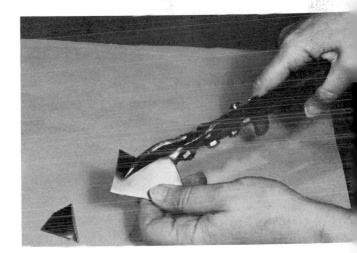

The pendant shape is cut out with metal shears.

Draw around the enameled shape and sketch a design for wire embedding.

With pliers or fingers, bend the wire to shape. Or you may prefer to design freely, without a pattern.

The wire is pounded on a steel block, for texture.

Brush the wire with a cleaning fluid and position it on the enameled pendant surface that has been covered with thick gum. Let it dry.

curvilinear, so more than one piece is needed to form sharp angles. Lines should be broken where they cross; otherwise a top crossover wire may snag and tear loose the part that is partially embedded. Loops of wire extending over the edge of an enameled shape should be used with caution; these loops can become bent and unsightly They may catch on objects if they project too far over the edge. Different weights of wire are sometimes incorporated into the same design. Lightweight wire, about 20- to 24-gauge, is satisfactory for small jewelry shapes. Heavier wire, 18- to 20-gauge, works well on tiles or trays.

There should be at least one layer of flux or other *transparent* enamel fired to the surface of a piece in which copper wire will be embedded. This is important because transparent enamel melts more quickly than opaque enamel, and it allows the wire to sink into it before heavy firescale collects on the wire and prevents fusion of enamel and copper. If you prefer to have an opaque background, fire a layer of flux over the opaque color before you apply the wire.

Metal must be free of oil and dirt, or enamel will not properly fuse to it when it is fired. This applies to wire as well as metal sheet. Even though the wire may have been cleaned once, most likely it will have become soiled by the fingers while the pattern was formed. To give it a final cleaning, brush it lightly with a soft watercolor brush that has been dipped into paint thinner or lighter fluid. Finally, dip it into full-strength gum, position it on the enameled copper shape, and allow it to dry.

Kiln heat must be kept up near 1500° F. while the wire is firing. It is advisable to heat the kiln to at least 1600° F. to allow for cooling when the door is opened. Position the copper piece on a trivet and put it into the hot kiln. When it becomes red-hot (in about three minutes), the wire will begin to sink into the enamel. If parts of the wire pattern seem to project above the surface of the enamel, hold the kiln door slightly open and tap down any protruding parts of the wire with a firing tool. It is important to wear an asbestos glove for this operation; bare skin exposed ever so briefly to 1500° F. heat can become painfully scorched. When the piece begins to turn red-hot, watch it closely so that it can be removed from the kiln before the wire sinks into the hot melted enamel and disappears. After the piece is removed from the kiln, allow it to cool slowly. Finally, rub the embedded wire and edges of the copper shape with steel wool to remove firescale and give the copper a soft sheen. Steel wool will not scratch enamels.

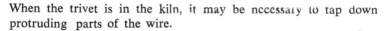

When the trivet is in the kiln, it may be necessary to tap down protruding parts of the wire.

Jewelry shapes with embedded wire.

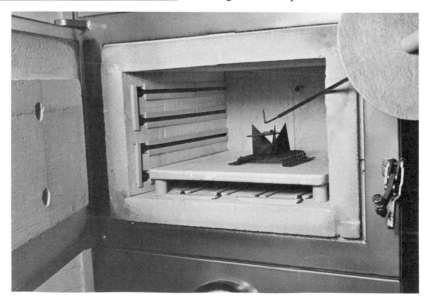

Pieces of rounded cathedral glass can be fired with wire.

If the wire is tapped down while in the kiln, avoid striking the piece of glass. It may stick to the tool.

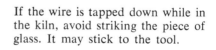

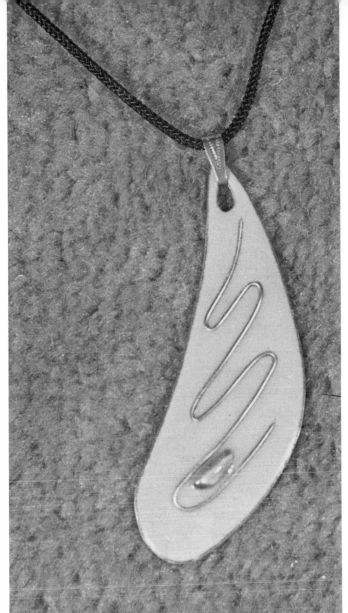

Turquoise pendant with copper wire and glass.

Stencil and wire on dark-green transparent enamel.

Large wire designs can be weighted down while the full-strength gum dries, so they will stay in place.

Pendant. Robert Engstrom. 14-gauge copper with silver inlay and Jet Line Black. Courtesy of the artist.

A single wire was shaped with fingers, then cleaned. Copper dots were punched from scrap metal.

Two bracelet sets. Robert Engstrom. Links are of 14 gauge copper. Transparent gray enamel has design of silver inlay and Jet Line Black. Courtesy of the artist. *Photo by Southwick-Andrews.*

CLOISONNÉ

Cloisonné, one of the oldest techniques in enameling, is still admired very much today. Contemporary craftsmen use the flat cloisonné wire for a silvery line in their composition. It may enclose individual colors, as it did historically, or it may be integrated into the design without strict separation of colors. In either case, the modern enamelist designs with it in terms of communicating a visual idea.

Early craftsmen soldered flat or square wires to a metal base, then filled spaces in between the wires with enamel. Today, very few craftsmen follow this tedious procedure. The wires are usually fused to a base coat of either transparent or opaque enamel. Spaces are filled with moist enamels to complete a design. Fine-silver wire in *18 by 30* B&S gauge is satisfactory for use on either enameled silver or copper.

A piece of fine silver should be cut with a jeweler's saw rather than with metal shears. For cutting small jewelry shapes, the 3-inch or 4-inch saw frame will do the job. For cutting more deeply, a 6-inch frame is useful. Saw blades for cutting silver are quite fragile and brittle. They must be handled with care. Loosen both the nuts on the saw frame and insert the blade all the way in, to the top jaw nut. The sawteeth should face away from the frame and angle toward the handle. Tighten the nut. Adjust the other nut so·the blade will fit into it about halfway. Brace the top of the frame against your hand or chest; compress the frame so the free end of the blade is pushed toward the second (or lower) nut; tighten the nut. Release the frame slowly so that it does not snap the blade. The blade must be taut in order to cut. Sawing can be done on a "V" board (cut from hardwood) clamped to the tabletop with a "C" clamp.

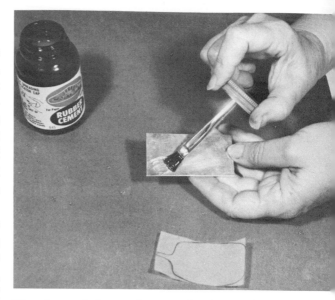

The shape of the pendant can be drawn directly on silver or it can be drawn on tracing paper that is cemented to the silver with rubber cement, as shown here. *Let the rubber cement dry.* If it is still damp, it will slide around while you are trying to saw it.

Put a little beeswax on the blade, and make a few preliminary strokes upward to form a starting groove. Pressure should be very light and only on the downward strokes.

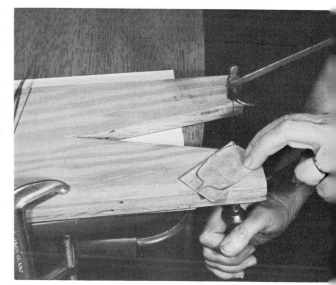

Bend the wires to conform with pattern lines. Each wire should include an angle or curve. Straight lengths of flat wire will not remain standing on edge but will fall flat when the piece is fired.

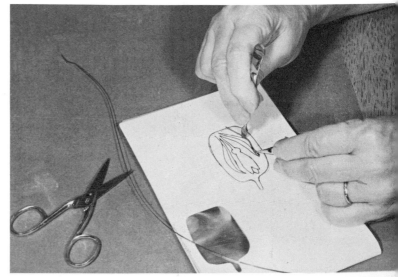

Dip each wire into full-strength gum, and position it on the enameled surface.

With a very small pointed brush, push each tiny ball of enamel into place between wires that have been fused to the base coat of enamel.

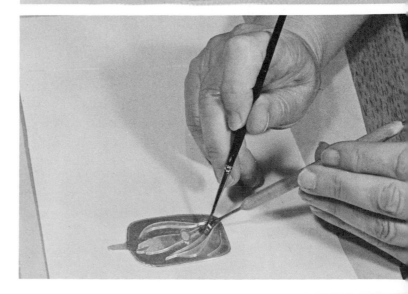

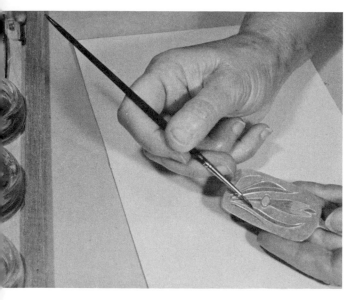

Pull the enamel back into narrow spaces with the damp brush. A final drop of water from the tip of the brush will flatten the enamel and carry it into hard-to-reach crevices.

With round-nosed pliers, the projection has been turned back for a loop. It is not enameled.

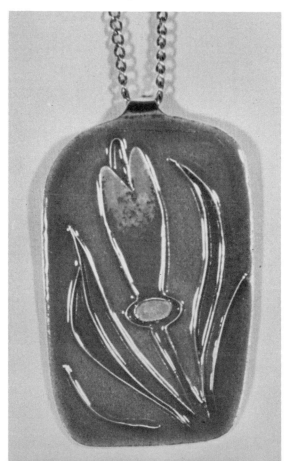

When a piece has been cut and edges have been filed and smoothed, draw a line design, keeping in mind that lines represent lengths of cloisonné wire that will be applied on edge. Wires can be annealed on asbestos board with a torch or on a clean firing rack in the kiln. Smooth the wire by drawing it tightly over a table edge. Cut it with sharp scissors or wire snips. Circles can be formed by bending the wire around small dowel sticks or nails. Sharp angles are made by pressing the wire over a metal straightedge. If fingers are employed to bend and manipulate the wires, protect them with tissues. Skin oil may prevent enamel from fusing to the silver.

Fire a layer of counterenamel to the back of the metal piece and a thin layer of enamel to the top surface. The surface enamel can be stoned thin if it seems thick or uneven. When all wires have been dipped into gum and positioned, dry them completely and fire the piece at 1450° F. until the wires have fused to the surface enamel. This may not take long, so watch carefully by opening the kiln door a crack from time to time. When the piece has been removed from the kiln, and cooled, it is time to apply colored enamels by the wet-inlay process.

Wash the separate colors and put them into shallow containers; glass coasters are fine for this. Add a few drops of agar or undiluted enameling gum to each moist color, and blend it well. When you change the colors, dip the brush and spatula into a container of water and dab them on a paper towel to clean them and prevent contamination of one color with another. When all areas of the design are completed, let the piece dry completely.

Fire it at a controlled temperature of 1450° F. until the enamel is shiny. The enamel will sink lower than the tops of the wires but will seem to climb up the sides of the wire. This is a very subtle effect, and is much admired by contemporary craftsmen. If, however, you want the enamel to be level with the top of the wires, apply one or more additional coats of enamel with firings in between. Stone the finished surface under water until enamel and wires are level. Dry the piece and give it a final short firing just long enough to restore gloss. For a duller, more satin finish, rub the final gloss with emery paste, clean the piece, and apply a wax that can be buffed.

There are other ways to develop a cloisonné design. Some craftsmen prefer to dip the wires into undiluted gum and set them directly on the metal surface. When the gum dries, enamel is sifted over wires and bare metal for the first firing. More enamel is applied to build up the design. Colors may be combined *within* individual cloisons instead of separating each color with a wire fence. Ends of wires are sometimes left free so color flows into the background color. This new attitude toward cloisonné has increased its appeal both among craftsmen and among collectors. It will always be admired because it has many interpretations. It can be lively or it can be serene; it can be dominant in a design or it can form texture in small amounts; it can be free and flowing or it can be intricate and refined. The simplest of patterns may be successfully attempted by the novice. The experienced craftsman enjoys displaying his skill in an elaborately conceived and expertly developed masterpiece.

NUN. Simple cloisonné. Hand-formed silver pendant. Courtesy of the American Art Clay Co.

PENGUIN. William Gehl. Orange-red on bright blue background, beige front. Courtesy of the American Art Clay Co.

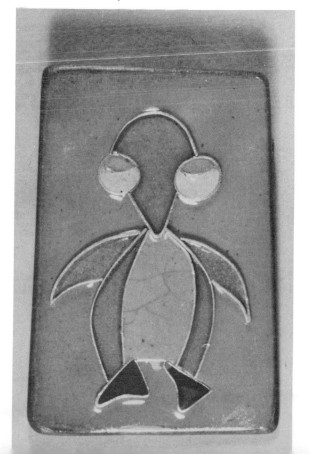

DEER. Nella Reichenberger. Hand-formed copper tray. White background with turquoise and blue cloisonné deer. Courtesy of the artist.

MOUNTAIN CLIMBERS. Audrea Kreye. Hand-constructed pewter paperweight. Sand was filled in at the top; then the cloisonné panel was cemented into place *within* a silver rim. Courtesy of the artist.

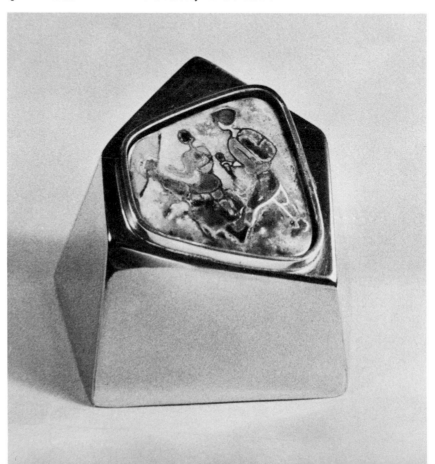

Brass box with cloisonné panel. Rama Webb. The domed copper panel has a base coat of flux. Gold wires were fused into place. Silver foil was applied and covered with transparent blues. Gold foil was applied under leaves, and surface was stoned to a matte finish. Courtesy of the artist.

EVE. Rama Webb. Delicate and sensitive rendering of the classic Eve. Silver cloisonné wires were set and fired to a base coat of dark-green enamel on domed copper. Opaques and transparents were built layer on layer with stoning and polishing. Courtesy of the artist.

Pendant. Phoebe and Harold Stabler. An oval cloisonné panel is set in a silver frame. Courtesy of the Cooper-Hewitt Museum of the Smithsonian Institution.

SPRING. Rama Webb. Cloisonné wires were fused to a base coat of transparent gold. Colors in wet inlay were blended together. The piece was stoned and polished for a matte finish. Courtesy of the artist.

MOMENTARY STOPOVER. Rama Webb. Fine silver wires were fused to a base coat. Opaques and transparents were applied in wet-inlay technique. Courtesy of the artist.

Mikado cloisonné bowl. Mary Sharp. A flux base was fired first. Mikado red was sifted and fired. Silver wires were gummed, set, and fused. Mikado enamel was *sifted overall,* and fused. Wires were stoned. A final firing restored the gloss. Courtesy of the artist.

Footed tray. Mary Sharp. Bright blue background contrasts with white and gray shaded sheep. Cloisons were filled by the wet-inlay technique. Courtesy of the artist.

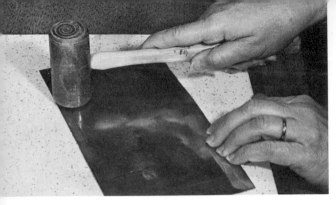

The copper tile is annealed, cleaned, and flattened. Edges are filed and rubbed with steel wool.

A design is scribed onto the bare copper. Asphaltum varnish is painted on the areas that will *not* be etched. Fingers must be kept off the bare copper.

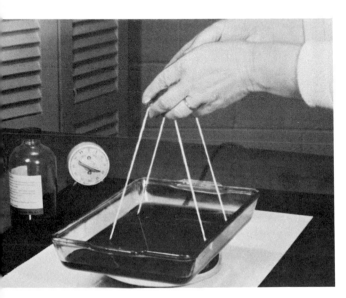

The glass dish is sitting on an electric trivet that supplies steady low heat. A timer keeps track of etching time for future reference.

CHAMPLEVÉ

Designs for champlevé enamel are chased, gouged, or etched into the metal, then inlaid with enamel. A typical champlevé design will have several areas of bare copper that contrast with enamel-inlaid areas. Opaque enamels in the strong colors and in black and white are particularly striking when they are inlaid against bare copper. The transparents do not have as much visual impact in champlevé work over copper; but in a closely related technique called *basse-taille,* an etched or engraved piece is completely covered with transparent enamel, and this can be quite handsome. Transparent enamels inlaid over silver are very effective.

Preliminary planning and sketching of the design are of special importance in this technique. By starting with a simple design that does not have many thin-line areas, the craftsman can gain an understanding of the process, then move on to work that is more elaborate.

Because thin layers of metal will be eaten away by acid in the etching process, in copper, 16-gauge metal is recommended. If fine silver is used for champlevé, 18-gauge will be adequate, because there is no firescale problem if some areas are inlaid quite thinly. Always anneal and clean the metal.

The areas that are *not* to be etched away are coated with asphaltum varnish or some other acid resist to protect them while the piece is in the acid bath. Another method is to cover the entire piece with asphaltum varnish, then, when it is nearly dry, scratch a design through to the metal. In either method, the exposed metal is eaten away by the acid. Asphaltum varnish can usually be ordered through a paint store.

Nitric acid diluted with water (one part acid to three parts water) makes a fairly fast etch. Many craft supply houses have other, safer, etching mordants that are not so hazardous to use. These mordants work faster if they are warm (not hot). An electric trivet makes a satisfactory warmer because it maintains a steady low temperature. Or the glass container that is used for the acid bath may be set in a pan of warm water; small amounts of hot water added occasionally to the pan of water keep it warm. If nitric acid is used, do not breathe the fumes. An electric fan will disperse them. Electroetching is a method by which the metal is eaten away with a combination of an electrolyte bath and very low amperage electric current. This is discussed later in the book.

When all surfaces of the piece to be etched have been cleaned and dried, transfer the design to the metal surface either by scribing it with a sharp tool or by tracing it with carbon paper. Because the copper must be completely free of oil when asphaltum varnish is applied, rest your hand on a tissue while you are applying the design.

The next step is to apply the asphaltum varnish over *areas that will not be etched*. These areas will be exposed copper (or silver) when the piece is completed. The brush should be a pointed one, and it must be cleaned from time to time with turpentine, then dried; this keeps the varnish flowing smoothly. A good procedure is to outline all design area edges first to keep them sharp, then fill in the rest of the background area. The coat should be smooth. Any pinholes that develop from bubbles in the varnish should be filled. The piece is left to dry a few hours; then it is turned over and covered carefully along the edges and the entire back with the asphaltum varnish or other acid resist. It can sit overnight or until it is nearly dry but still slightly tacky. If it dries out completely, the resist may peel off in spots.

Two glass trays are prepared for the etching process; one is for clear rinsing water, the other is for the etching solution. If nitric acid is used, acid must be poured

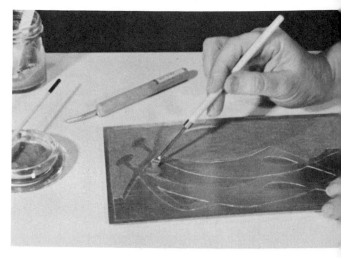

Moist porcelain-blue opaque is packed into all areas that have been etched.

THE DANCERS. The enamel was stoned flat to the level of the bare copper areas. Darker blue wet *painting* enamel was rubbed over it to give texture. Black overglaze lines were brushed around the edges of enamel areas. A final quick firing restored gloss. Copper areas were cleaned and buffed.

A silver pin made from two identical shapes cut from 22-gauge sheet silver. Openings were sawed in one piece; then the two pieces were soldered together with hard silver solder. Recesses were then filled with shades of blue opaque in the champlevé method.

Champlevé trays. Audrea Kreye. Asphaltum varnish was *trailed* over the copper trays for unique designing. They were etched, and low areas were filled with enamels. Bare copper areas on tray at left were oxidized; bare copper areas on tray at right were polished. Courtesy of the artist.

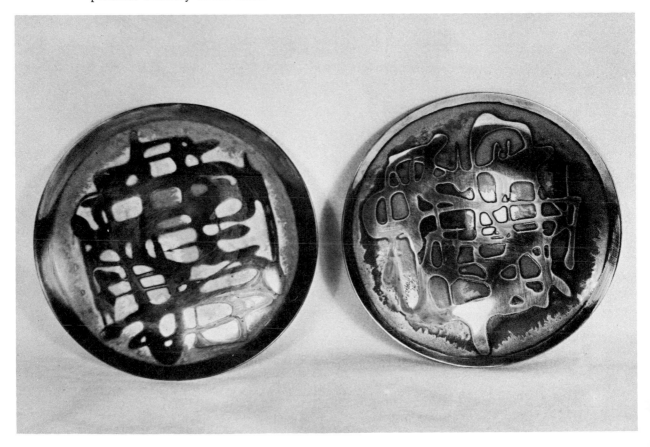

Pyx, French, twelfth century. Enamel on bronze champlevé. Many of these religious reliquaries were made for the Church. "Pyx" was the name given to the box in which the reserved Host was carried to the sick. William Randolph Hearst Collection. Courtesy of the Los Angeles County Museum.

into water; if water is poured into acid, it will sputter and cause problems. Acid should not come into contact with the skin. Two loops of soft string slipped under the metal piece like a cradle are used for lifters. The piece is lowered into the acid bath *face down* to allow disintegrating particles of copper to float down and away from the etched area. String loops are shifted sideways from time to time so they do not interfere with the etching process; otherwise thin, partially etched lines will be left where strings are in contact with metal. Prop one end of the piece on a small block of wood so acid can reach all parts of the design. If the acid bath is too strong and fast-cutting, it will undercut design edges.

Only experience can dictate the length of etching time, because it depends on the temperature and strength of the acid solution. The piece is lifted from its acid bath at frequent intervals, then lowered by means of the string loops into the glass tray of clear water. Examine carefully with the fingernail tips to measure the etched depth. It is difficult to measure an etched depth in fractions of an inch. When the etching has enough depth to receive an adequate layer of enamel, withdraw the piece, rinse it, and remove all the asphaltum varnish with a rag and turpentine. Clean the piece in the usual way and *counterenamel it.* Keep the counterenamel thin if the piece is a flat panel or tile, or bare copper areas on the surface will cause the piece to warp.

Enamel is applied to the etched areas in the wet-inlay method. Pile it slightly higher than the metal surface. It may be necessary to apply a second coat if etching is deep. Dry it *completely,* and fire it at a steady temperature of 1450° F. When it is removed from the kiln, and cooled, clean and polish bare metal areas, and stone the enamel under water with a fine emery stone until it is level and smooth. A final firing at 1400° F. restores gloss to the enamel.

Pyx. Mary Sharp. This complex piece was inspired by thirteenth century reliquaries. Triangular panel—Angel who appeared to Mary; Alpha and Omega; rectangular end panel—shepherds seeing the star signaling Christ's birth; front top panel—the resurrection; lower long panel—Mary and Joseph with the Christ Child on their flight into Egypt. This handsome champlevé enamel box is gold-plated. Courtesy of the artist.

Horizon Breakthrough. Large mural constructed on several levels. Gail Kristensen.

Mural. Enamels combined with copper scale. Paul Hultberg.

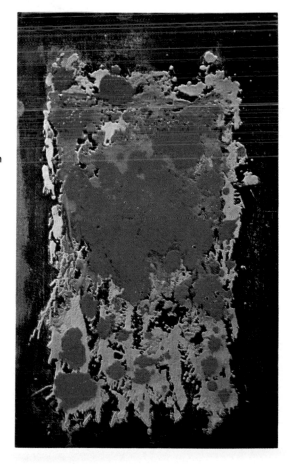

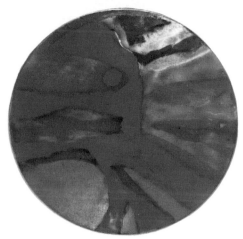

Abstract Red. Large tray. Linda Gebert.

Candle holder. Constructed of pewter sheet with enameled fine silver drip pads. Audrea Kreye.

Sun Worshipper. Enameled copper and wood appliqué. Polly Rothenberg.

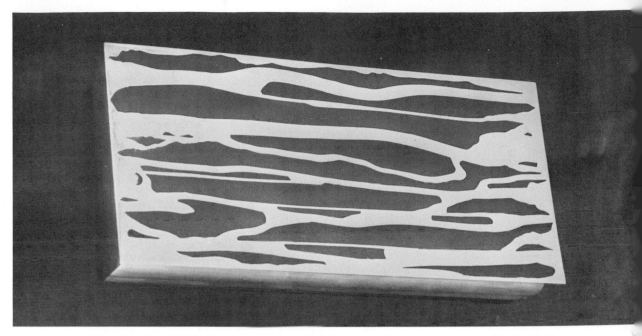

Champlevé panel. Mary Sharp. The panel was etched and inlaid with imperial blue; then it was silver-plated. Courtesy of the artist.

Champlevé panel. Mary Sharp. When the design had been painted with asphaltum varnish and etched 1/16 of an inch, it was cleaned, then filled with enamels in the wet-inlay method. They were dried, fused, and stoned level. A final firing restored gloss. Exposed metal was cleaned and *engraved*. Courtesy of the artist.

Champlevé bowl. Justin Brady. Etched depressions were filled with enamel, and fired. Courtesy of the American Art Clay Co.

Brass-plated champlevé box. Mary Sharp. Courtesy of the artist.

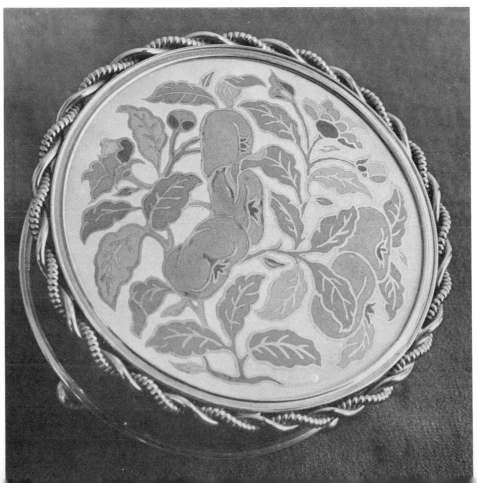

BASSE-TAILLE

The manipulation of a metal breaks up its surface plane. Light can be refracted and reflected through a covering coat of transparent enamel to add variations and iridescence to its color. Any method of working the metal that is to be *enameled* can be called "basse-taille" (pronounced *bahs tah'-ee*). It is a French term meaning "low-cut."

Embossing and chasing are perhaps the best known and simplest ways to manipulate the metal surface. Embossing is a pattern in relief made by pressing or hammering on the reverse side of metal; chasing is the indenting of the top metal surface with hammer and tools, but without a cutting edge. In repoussé, patterns are usually worked from both sides of the metal, which may be any weight from 36-gauge foil to 18-gauge sheet copper or preformed copper shape. The pieces of heavier weight are affixed in a pan of pitch that has been slightly heated. The metal is *worked* or tooled in any manner that gives the desired result. There are no "rules" for repoussé.

For smooth, continuous lines, start with a tracing tool. Slant the top away from you at such an angle that, when the tool is struck, it moves toward you to make a smooth continuous groove. Strike the tool with the flat end of a chasing hammer or small ball peen hammer. Any kind of tool that does the job is fine. From time to time as the metal is worked it will stiffen. It must be annealed to restore malleability.

A heavy cast-iron pitch bowl is supported on a rubber disk. It is tilted to the most convenient position. Play the propane torch over the pitch to just soften it. It should *not* be hot enough to run.

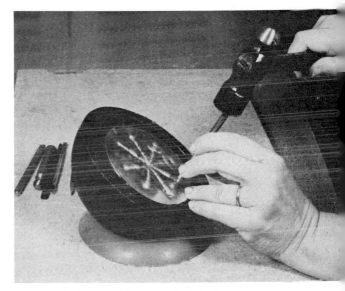

An annealed disk with a penciled design is pressed into the pitch, which comes over the edge in two or three places. A variety of tools is used to work the metal. Two fingers brace against the pitch pot. If necessary, anneal the metal from time to time.

The finished repoussé box top is covered with transparent olive-green enamel fired to both sides at 1500° F.

Tin cans are excellent for storing pitch. They can be set on top of a hot kiln to soften the pitch. In order to chase the exterior of a bowl, fill it with pitch and support it on a sandbag.

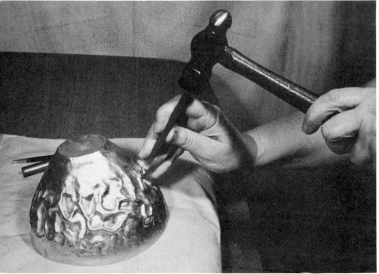

An *annealed* hand-raised bowl has been filled with pitch. When the bowl was formed, a bulge was left around the bowl's middle section. It is worked from the outside only. All tool marks are left in the metal for texture, and are not removed by planishing.

The pitch was softened in the bowl and removed when the chasing was completed. The remainder was burned out in the kiln. It turns to soft white ash. The piece is cleaned and enameled with transparent gold. A half-inch sifter gets enamel into nooks and crannies. Fire at 1500° F.

Deep copper shapes are filled with soft pitch that soon becomes firm as it cools. It forms an excellent resilient support for the metal that is to be worked. The bowl is supported on a sandbag, and its surface is manipulated with a variety of tools. If the pitch hardens, it can be softened by playing a torch lightly over the bowl's exterior or by setting the bowl in a pan of very hot water.

When all chasing is complete, the bowl is set on top of a hot kiln to resoften the pitch. The pitch is dug out and returned to a pitch can. To clean the bowl of remaining pitch, paint the bowl's exterior with Scale-off or Amacote, and put it into the hot kiln. The pitch will burn out in a cloud of smoke that soon dissipates and harms nothing. Only a soft gray ash will remain in the copper bowl. Pitch can also be burned out with a torch. When the bowl has been cleaned in the usual way, it is ready to be enameled.

Craftsmen who specialize in basse-taille enameling usually develop their own methods of working the metal. Flat panels are supported on a variety of resilient surfaces. Thin 36 gauge copper foil can be worked over a magazine or on a sandbag. The design

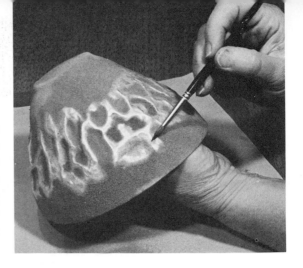

Transparent olive-green is sifted all over and is *dried*. The green enamel is removed from raised areas with a soft brush. The piece is fired at 1450° F.

is drawn directly onto the metal with a pencil or scored with a scriber. The piece is usually worked from the back side first, then it is refined by chasing the front surface. When the completed piece is cleaned and enameled on both surfaces, it is ready for mounting on a background. The back side is filled in with plaster or with a wonderful material called *joint cement,* obtainable at builders' supply stores. When it dries, this fill-in material will hold the thin enameled panel firm so it cannot be pushed in and cracked after it has been mounted.

Basse-taille bowl. Polly Rothenberg. The interior is enameled in transparent turquoise fired at 1550° F.

For more refined effects in basse-taille, metal is engraved or etched before it is covered with enamel. The metal is cut so that tiny facets catch and reflect subtle glints of light. Engraving with a variety of gravers is a fine art requiring skill, practice, and especially patience. However, simple patterns can be created with a vibrating engraver. The metal surface is cut and roughened to provide those tiny points of reflective texture that display transparent enamels so exotically. Designs etched with acid as described for champlevé may also be completely covered with transparent enamels.

An electric vibrating engraver makes a cross-hatched pattern on a silver pendant. The piece is anchored with tape.

The silver pendant is covered with light-green transparent enamel.

Oval bowl. Polly Rothenberg. The pattern was traced with pencil and cut with a vibrating engraver. All lines are formed of tiny cross-hatching to give the maximum amount of sparkle when it is covered with transparent gold and brown. Collection of Mr. and Mrs. Edwin Oxner, San Jose, California.

Silver repoussé enamel tray. Collection of Justin Brady, Indianapolis, Indiana. Courtesy of the American Art Clay Co.

Holy font bowl. Lillian Skaggs. Raised, chased bowl in transparent red. Celtic cross detail in transparent gold. Courtesy of the artist.

Enameled box lid. Mae Conner. Repoussé on 36-gauge tooled copper foil. Courtesy of Thomas C. Thompson Co.

ESCAPE. Elinor Helitzer. Etched enameled panel, 9 inches by 12 inches. Courtesy of the artist.

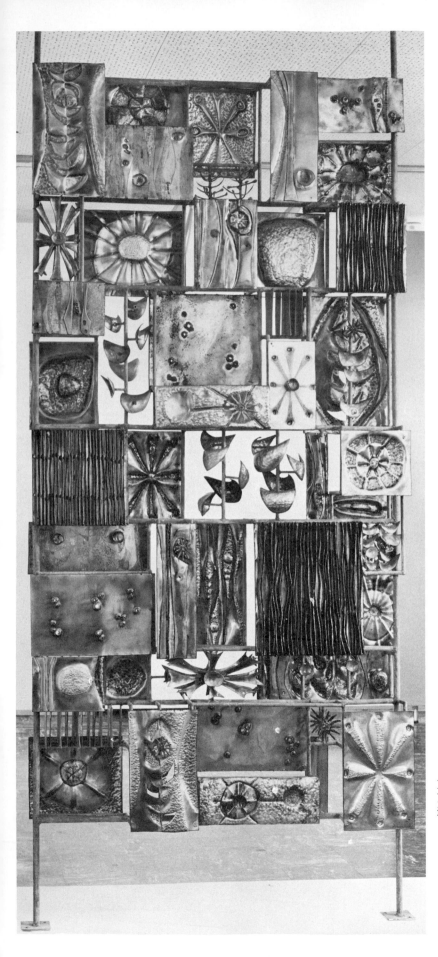

Divider. Dextra and Charles Frankel. Courtesy of the artists. Photo by Richard Gross.

Basse-taille panel. June Schwarcz. Concave panel framed in aluminum. Electroformed lines of varying thicknesses are enameled in transparent enamels. Courtesy of the artist.

Silver bowl. Claire Strauss. Shallow etched and enameled bowl on a low foot, in basse-taille. Courtesy of Cooper-Hewitt Museum, Smithsonian Institution.

Triptych. Richard Loving. Enamel over hammered copper, with symbolic floating human figures. Mr. Loving teaches in the School of the Art Institute of Chicago. Courtesy of the artist.

Early twentieth-century Japanese vase. Great skill and craftsmanship are evident in this delicate Oriental plique-à-jour. In this technique, extremely fine silver or gold wires build up a design on enameled metal. The spaces are filled with additional enamel, in the wet-inlay process, similar to cloisonné. Finally acid is poured into the piece to etch away the metal lining, leaving only enamel and wires. Collection of Helen and Kathryn Pinkney, Dayton, Ohio.

PLIQUE-À-JOUR

Although the processes of plique-à-jour have remained little changed for centuries, the designs, like those of cloisonné, have assumed an airy informality. The techniques have relaxed to some extent, in keeping with the artistic freedom of our time. In plique-à-jour, enamel is melted within surrounding frames of metal-like little stained-glass windows. The metal is usually fine silver; copper can cause firescale problems.

For one method, a design is developed that can be fragmented into tiny apertures that are no wider than ⅛-inch. However, they can be longer, preferably no more than an inch. Shaped openings are sawed in a piece of sheet silver with a jeweler's saw. The piece is laid flat, and the openings are packed

Plique-à-jour bird. Patricia Slaughter. Ends of flat wires are casually lapped in the new free interpretation of this technique. This exquisite little bird is freestanding. Courtesy of the artist.

with either gum-moistened 80-mesh transparent enamel or small particles of very low-fusing transparent lumps. The 80-mesh enamels should be washed for true transparency. Stray grains of enamel are cleaned from the bare metal surrounding the packed holes.

Start with a few small shaped slots for a very simple design. Once you have conquered the technique, it is easy to add more apertures for a more complicated design. Use a sharp nail to center-punch a dent that will anchor your drill bit. Drill a tiny hole through which you will thread the saw blade. Fasten it into the saw frame as described under "Cloisonné." Saw out each hole carefully.

If the openings are filled with bits of lump enamel, the piece is fired flat on mica. One firing of the lumps is usually sufficient to fill an opening. If 80-mesh enamel is tamped into the holes, it will shrink as it melts, and more enamel must be packed, and refired. When filled with ground enamel, firing can be flat on mica or the piece can be fired in a vertical position by being suspended from nichrome wire stuck into insulating brick. Bend a little hook in the upper end of the wire. Another way to support the piece vertically is to stand it in a small groove cut into the insulating brick. As the enamel melts, capillary attraction will hold it in place for a limited length of time. Then it will begin to sag. The first firings will usually pull the enamel away from an edge or leave a hole in the center. These holes can be filled and given another firing. Some interesting effects have been created by incorporating the openings formed by the "pullaway" into the design.

Ovals are formed with bezel wire and silver solder. A hole is drilled in one end of each oval. A wooden dowel is slipped under the drill point to support the oval in a small vise.

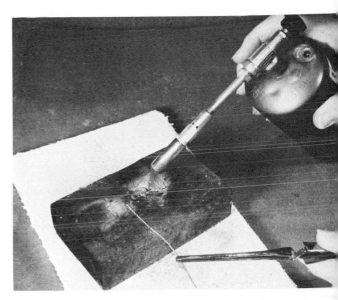

Fine silver wire is held under the torch flame until it forms a little ball on each end. The wire is cut in two halves.

One wire is strung through the drilled hole in each silver oval, with the ball end on the inside. The ovals are laid flat on mica and filled with *soft-fusing* transparent lumps (the kind used for scrolling) that fuse at about 1350° F. They are fused on the mica, supported on a mesh firing rack or a piece of soft insulating brick.

In another method of plique-à-jour, elaborate open designs are formed with bezel wire, and either transparent 80-mesh enamel or very soft low-fusing transparent lumps are packed into the spaces. They are fired on mica. Larger openings can be used successfully if the soft-fusing lumps are applied.

The method of firing from a vertical position gives a shiny surface to both sides of the enamel "window." Firing on mica leaves a slight texture on the underside where the enamel is in contact with mica. However, a final quick firing in a suspended position will give a gloss to the textured side of enamels fired on mica.

Each wire is cut short and curved to form a small ring, which is attached to a fine silver chain suspended from an earring finding. Fused enamel holds the wire securely. Colorless lumps were fused, then light-blue enamel was sprinkled over for a second firing.

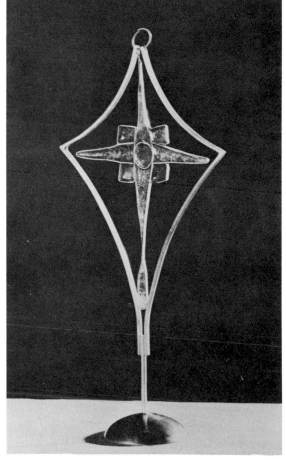

Plique-à-jour cross. Justin Brady. Courtesy of the American Art Clay Co.

Plique-à-jour silver pendant. Polly Rothenberg. Green and chartreuse enamel. Fired "in the air," suspended on wire. Collection of Helen Pinkney.

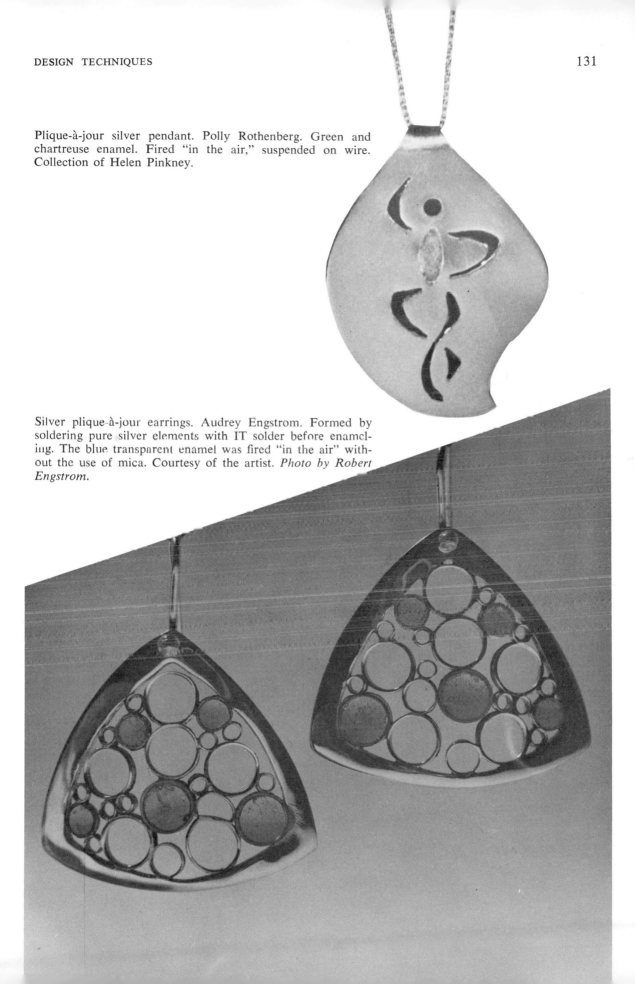

Silver plique-à-jour earrings. Audrey Engstrom. Formed by soldering pure silver elements with IT solder before enameling. The blue transparent enamel was fired "in the air" without the use of mica. Courtesy of the artist. *Photo by Robert Engstrom.*

Silver plique-à-jour pendant. Audrey Engstrom. Elements of
fine silver and sterling were forged and soldered. Enamel is
yellow. Courtesy of the artist. *Photo by Robert Engstrom.*

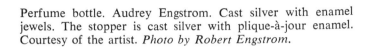

Perfume bottle. Audrey Engstrom. Cast silver with enamel jewels. The stopper is cast silver with plique-à-jour enamel. Courtesy of the artist. *Photo by Robert Engstrom.*

Stemmed sweetmeat dish. Masriera y Carreras, Barcelona, Spain. This fabulous plique-à-jour piece is brightly multi-colored, depicting couples dancing in a landscape near a windmill. Base is champlevé of grapes, vine, and leaves. Courtesy of Cooper-Hewitt Museum, Smithsonian Institution.

ENAMELED SCULPTURE

The broad planes and simple lines of enameled sculpture differ from those of welded, forged, or cast forms. Surfaces are indented, textured, and twisted to give the action and three-dimensional quality necessary for maximum light and color reflection; thus the beauty of enamels is displayed to best advantage. A twisted piece that has one light surface and one dark side may be very exciting. Light and dark surfaces show here and there, now turning a curve, now disappearing, with perhaps just a line of color showing between two planes of the contrasting side. Metal and enamel are in harmony.

It is wise to begin with a single piece of metal for simple sculpture projects until you have acquired some dexterity in soldering. Very interesting figures can be formed from one piece of metal. A human shape with tapering hands and feet may be pounded, textured, curved, and bent into a standing, dancing, or reclining posture.

Draw the figure on a piece of heavy drawing paper. Cut, bend, and manipulate it to find just the right shape and posture so the final piece will be in balance. Smooth out the paper pattern again and place it flat on the copper sheet so it can be traced directly onto the metal. Cut most of the excess copper from the traced design with metal shears. Refine the shape with a jeweler's saw and files. Smooth it with steel wool.

The next step is to anneal the copper piece so it will be malleable. Then it can be pounded and given texture with a small ball peen or chasing hammer to give strength and contour to the shape and add to the three-dimensional quality. As soon as the copper has been bent into the desired form, it is cleaned thoroughly in readiness for enameling.

A twisted metal shape has a slight tendency to straighten out when it is subjected to heat, so apply enamel to the underneath and concealed areas first; then carefully tie a piece or two of thin iron binding wire around the outside of bent parts to help hold the metal in shape during the first firing. Remove the wire for subsequent firings, because the fired enamel will hold the metal firm.

When a sculptured piece is put into the kiln to be fired, only the edges should touch the trivet. Pieces of nichrome wire stuck into insulating brick give added support to large or awkward shapes.

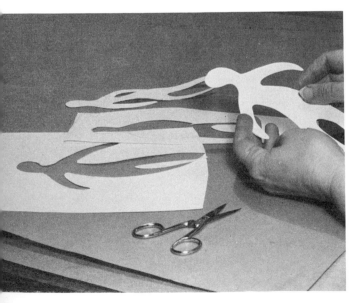

Simple shapes are cut from cardboard and manipulated into various postures.

The pattern is traced on 18-gauge copper with a scriber. It is cut out with metal shears.

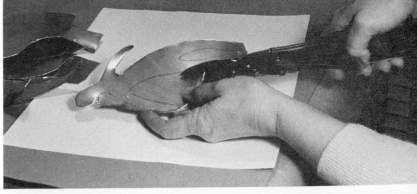

All copper shapes are annealed; then they are hammered for texture. If they are bent so they balance, they will have a balanced appearance.

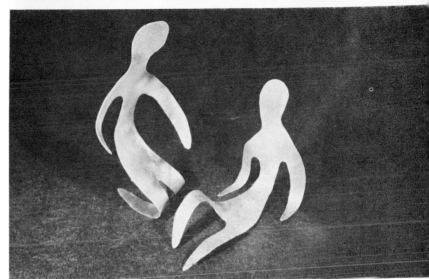

The figures are enameled in golden-brown transparent in front and opalescent white on their backs.

Although this piece looks complicated, it is in one piece.

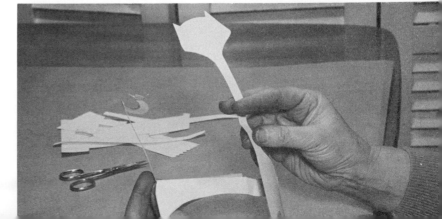

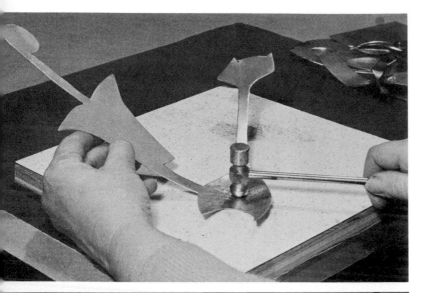

The pattern is scribed on 18-gauge sheet copper, cut with metal shears, and refined with files. It is pounded all over for texture, strength, and shape.

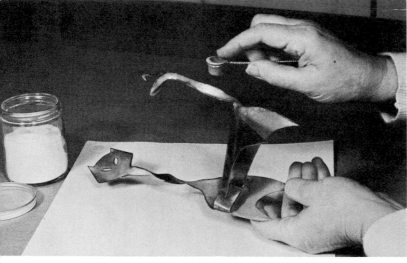

Tiny sifters are useful for reaching small concealed areas. Notice the flange that bends back to join with the front body section.

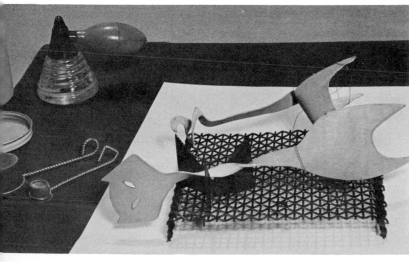

Binding wire holds the piece in shape while enamel on concealed surfaces is fired. Only edges should touch the firing rack. A small trivet supports the neck.

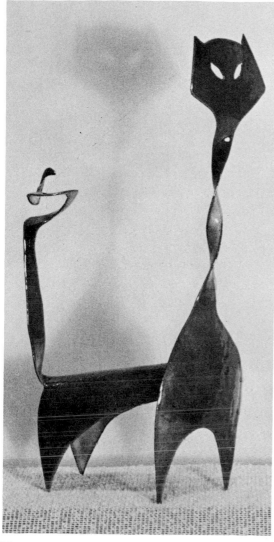

The transparent brown and opaque chartreuse figure stands firm and balanced.

Christmas tree. Nella Reichenberger. Free-swinging panels are mounted on brass coils. Lump enamel and stained-glass jewels are fused to various bright enamel colors. Courtesy of the artist.

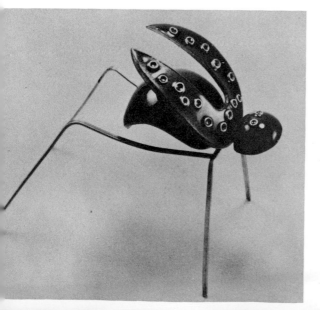

Constructed insect. Justin Brady. The head is ruby-red transparent; the wings are green transparent. Body is blue over red to form plum color. The pieces were fired separately, then bolted together through drilled holes. Large enameled sculptures could be formed by this method. Courtesy of American Art Clay Co.

THE BIRD. Treva Runyon. Formed from 16-gauge copper. The eyes are enameled copper washers. Colors are bright blue, green, and white. Courtesy of the artist.

BLUE FISHBOWL. Treva Runyon. A ten-inch suspended disk has mobile fish within fish. They cast interesting shadows. Enamels are transparent deep blues and greens with accents of transparent enamel jewels over silver foil. Courtesy of the artist. *Photo by Audio Visual Service.*

Copper fountain, enamel forms. Dextra and Charles Frankel. Water flows over enameled copper forms. The bronze casting for water flow is of lost-wax-process casting. The reciprocation pump, with nine outlets and controls for each outlet, regulates the water's height. The self-contained fountain is 8 feet long by 3 feet wide, with a 2-inch lip. The fountain's sides are of copper repoussé in marine forms. The fountain was made for and installed in the court of Pacific View Memorial Park, Newport Beach, California. Courtesy of the artists. *Photo by Richard Gross.*

ENAMEL PAINTINGS AND PORTRAITS

It is still occasionally customary to put all enameling that is not separated by wires or sunk into gouged or etched cavities into the category of Limoges enamels. The enamel craftsmen of Limoges, France, in the fifteenth century, departed from those earlier methods for the first time. They were the innovative artists of their day. Enamels were fired over enamels; foils were applied; and realistic enamel paintings blossomed and flourished all over France.*

In America there was no tradition in enameling, so American enamels developed with a creative spontaneity that still exists. There are American enamelists who admire and practice skillfully and beautifully the intricate enamel disciplines of the pre-Renaissance period. It is hoped they will continue to keep alive these impressive and precious techniques, while others move on to new expressions.

Enamel is being discovered and exploited by an increasing number of painters of our time, who see in its enduring qualities a material that neither fades nor deteriorates. It has another dimension; it has lustrous depth unattainable with paint pigments. When light changes, luminous color glows and recedes, giving warmth and character and mounting shadows with endless variations long after the painting has been completed.

The working methods of enamel painters are as varied as their approaches to painting. Gail Kristensen is a painter, sculptor, ceramist, and enamel craftsman. Her large enamel murals are constructed on several planes. Her enamel portraits are life-size character paintings. Although she works from a sketch, she applies enamels freely, much as she would put paint over a canvas. She may sift enamel evenly or push it

* Kenneth Bates, *The Enamelist* (Cleveland and New York: The World Publishing Co., 1967), pp. 22–24.

around with fingers or brush to get the desired effect.

Portraits

A comparatively recent development in enamel painting is the resurgence of enamel portraiture. Rather than photographic likeness, such as the French Limoges artists produced, portrait painters are finding enamels remarkably well suited to dynamic character portrayal. In general, contemporary works are quite large, but an occasional small portrait is seen.

Paintings can be created with dusted and trailed 80-mesh enamels or with fine-mesh liquid painting enamels. The latter come in tubes, and are applied much in the manner of oil paints. Because they are enamel, not pigment, there are some differences that must be taken into account. Where pigments can be blended, painting enamel tends to collect into little blobs, if one painted color is blended over another. It is best to paint a layer of color, then fire it. The next layer is smoothly applied over the first, and so on, firing in between each application.

First counterenamel the copper panel, and fire a base coat of transparent enamel to the top surface. This can be either flux or a light color. When the piece has cooled, outline the chief mass areas of the painting or portrait with fine-mesh painting enamel in a color that will be used in the picture. As the painting develops, this sketch will blend in with the colors. Fire the sketched lines onto the base coat of enamel. Firing temperatures for fine-mesh painting enamels are very important. Have the kiln hot, about 1550° F., when the piece is put into it. Let the temperature drop to about 1400° F. Withdraw the piece as soon as the enamel turns shiny. These fine-mesh enamels can easily overfire.

Any liquid *black* enamel, either overglaze, underglaze, or black painting enamel, will deteriorate and sink into the base coat *if it is overfired*. This characteristic does not seem so pronounced in other liquid enamel colors.

Although liquid enamels do not blend easily when they are being applied, they can be blended *before* they are used. Light tints and mixed colors can be achieved on the palette. Begin by laying in the darker color areas in the painting, then paint medium and light areas, with firings in between. Both white-bristle oil brushes and camel's-hair or sable brushes are useful in developing an enamel painting. The fine-mesh enamel tends to collect on the brush, and must be removed by being dipped in turpentine. Do not be discouraged if your first enamel painting seems to get messy and blurred. It takes a little practice to get the *feel* of this medium,

but the results can be so rewarding, they are well worth the effort required.

When all the mass areas and shadings have been applied and fired, it is time to apply the definitive fine black lines. They are applied with a small sable brush. Let the painting enamel dry completely before any firing. The drying can be speeded by thrusting the piece quickly in and out of the hot kiln, a procedure that is not advisable with 80-mesh or coarser enamels. Once you feel you have finished your enamel painting, do not work it over, as is sometimes done with an oil picture. The painting will begin to deteriorate when fired too many times. An enamel painting looks best if it is freely executed and not worked over.

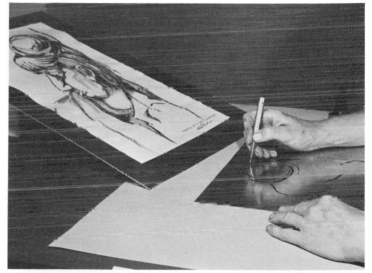

Gail Kristensen sketches in mass areas directly on the clean copper panel with a brush and India ink (which fires away in the first firing). Lines are scored over the ink drawings with a metal scriber.

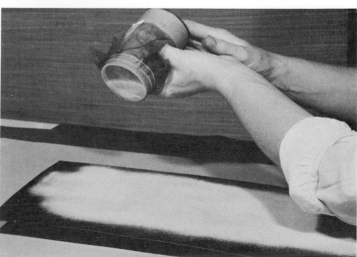

The panel is covered with flux, and fired. The piece is counterenameled.

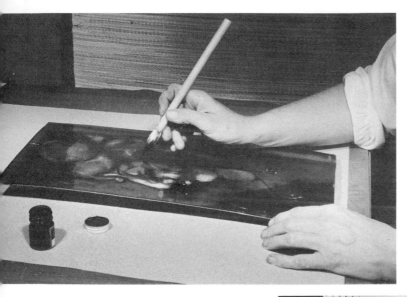

Various transparent colors are dusted over the sketched lines, which are clearly visible through the fired flux. Black ink lines have vanished, but the scored lines remain. With a pointed Oriental watercolor brush and Fine Line Black, details are added and fired.

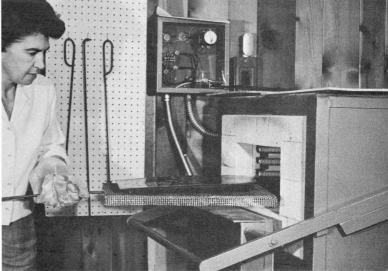

Gail Kristensen's kiln is a large one with a door that slides down. It is constructed so the door is controlled with light pressure.

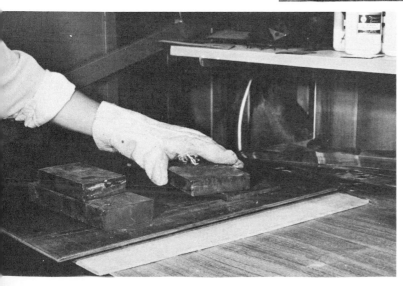

The red-hot panel is removed from the kiln, placed on a heavy sheet of asbestos board, and covered with a sheet of heavy steel and steel blocks to prevent warpage.

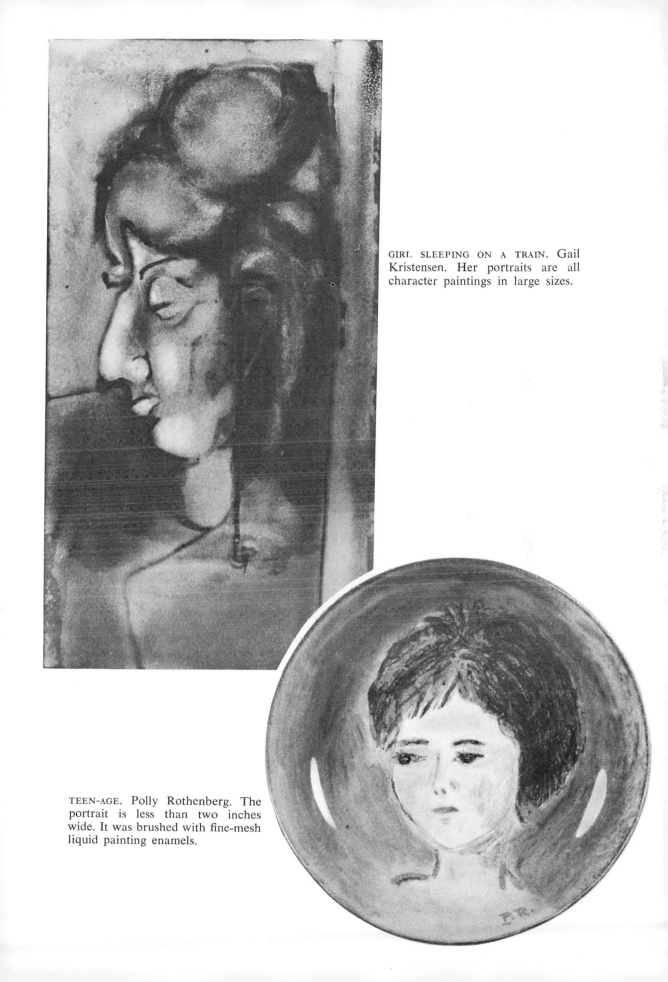

GIRL SLEEPING ON A TRAIN. Gail Kristensen. Her portraits are all character paintings in large sizes.

TEEN-AGE. Polly Rothenberg. The portrait is less than two inches wide. It was brushed with fine-mesh liquid painting enamels.

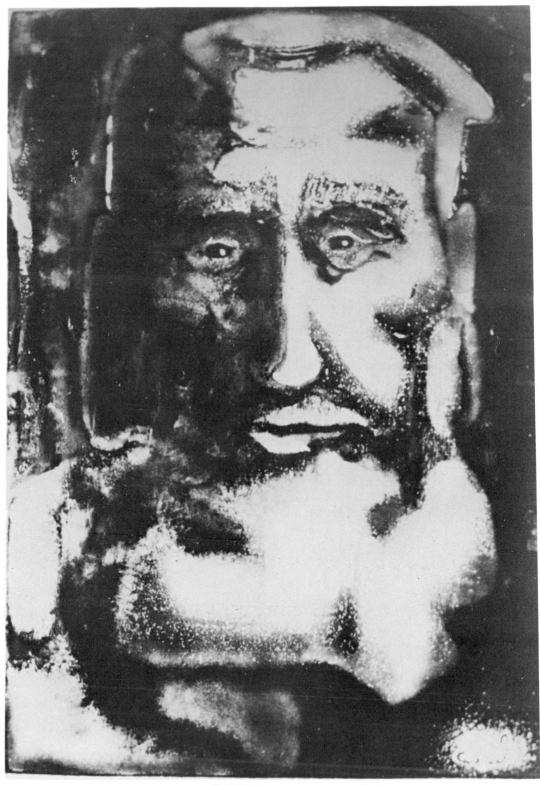

THE WISE ONE. Gail Kristensen. Courtesy of the artist.

Mary Sharp at work in her studio. Mary Sharp's enamels are detailed and refined. With patience and skill, she creates and teaches an amazing variety of both modern and traditional techniques.

BLONDE GIRL. Mary Sharp. The girl's eyes, lips, and nostrils are done in underglaze over tracings on bare copper. Flux was applied. Hair areas were given a coat of light yellow; the background is red. Firings were 1500° F. Shading and details were painted and blended with liquid enamel and fired at 1100° F. Courtesy of the artist.

CAT. Mary Sharp. The cat's head is a mixture of colors that approximate fur texture. The piece was fired, and details were added with fine-mesh enamels. Courtesy of the artist.

GRISAILLE PORTRAIT. Mary Sharp. This fine character piece is an example of a classic technique that is enjoying a revival of interest. Courtesy of the artist.

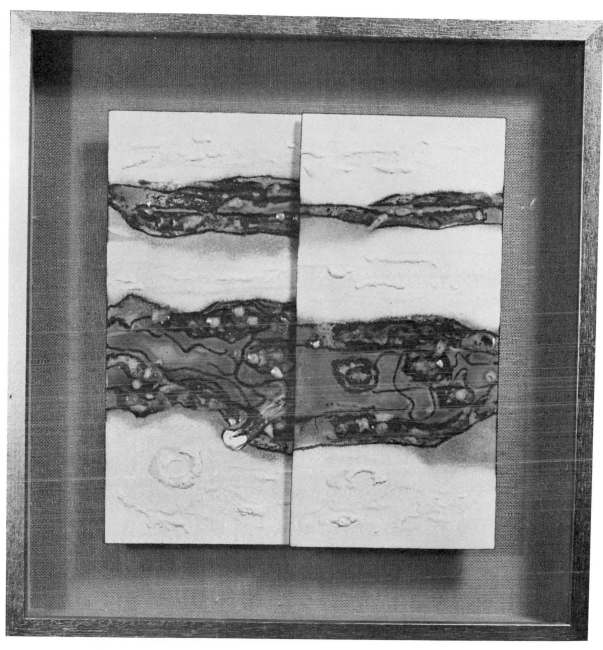

SCAPE. Elinor Helitzer. Small mural on two levels. Stencil, dusting, and wet inlay. Courtesy of the artist.

PROCESSION OF ROYALS. Norman Magden. Courtesy of The Butler Institute of American Art.

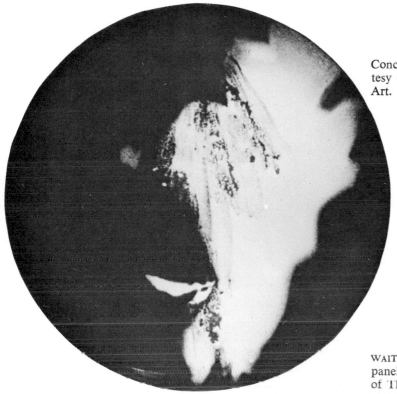

Concave panel. Barbara Coffman. Courtesy of The Butler Institute of American Art.

WAITING. Ruth Markus. Sensitive enamel panel in wet-inlay technique. Courtesy of The Butler Institute of American Art.

An 18-gauge sheet of copper was enameled on both sides with flux. Transparent yellow-gold and golden-brown were dusted freely over the top surface, and fired. Face and hair are sketched in with brown painting-enamel, and fired.

Hair and some shadows are applied in brown painting enamel with a white-bristle oil painting brush. Piece is fired at 1400° F.

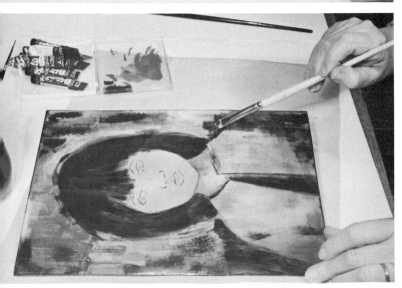

Dark areas are applied in bright colors of purple, red, blue, and brown. Form is developed and brought forward by painting dark around the lighter face and light around the dark hair; this also begins to develop some third dimension. Piece is fired.

DESIGN TECHNIQUES

Light red-brown is brushed over the background and applied as shadows on the face. Eye sockets are developed with some detail in eyes. Bright background colors are allowed to show through the overpainting. All firings are 1400° F.

Black details are brushed with small sable brush. Highlights in face are emphasized with ivory. Piece is fired.

CITY CHILD. Polly Rothenberg.

Experimental Enameling

AN APPROACH TO EXPERIMENTAL ENAMELING

Enamel is being exploited by imaginative artists whose new processes and bold designs take advantage of the basic properties of heat, metal, and silicates. Traditionally, metals have been pounded, punched, engraved, etched, chased, and cut. The experimentalist welds, brazes, solders, casts, and electroforms metals before further enhancing them with enamels; sometimes he treats both metal and enamel with additives for unusual effects.

The enamelist may draw from industry and become as involved with its discoveries and widening horizons as contemporary sculptors who take entire machines and strip, dismantle, or pillage them for whatever suits their creative needs. The craftsman who accepts change both within and beyond a traditional framework and who experiments in the spirit of "anything goes" may, at first, find himself carried forward into absurdity. However, he should soon be bombarded with new and evocative design ideas. He may finally extract that which is new and useful to him, without completely relinquishing all that is fine and enduring from the past.

Copper Firescale Patterns

When bare copper is heated to 1500° F. for one or more times, a black encrustation builds up on the surface of the metal; it is commonly called *firescale*. If the piece is fired several times, variations occur according to temperature variations in the kiln.

When the copper is left too long in the kiln, or at a much higher temperature, a dense black surface will cover the metal and be difficult to remove. If the temperature is lower than 1500° F., often most of the variations fire away and disappear in ensuing firings. Copper firescale forms patterns that are quite exciting when they are incorporated into a design. This is an interesting area for experimentation.

After a piece is removed from the kiln and is cool, use a medium-firm brush to whisk away loose particles of the copper scale. Some of it will pop loose as the copper cools. A transparent enamel can be fired over the still-attached scale for an interesting textured background on which to build a design. Beautiful reds, greens, black, gold, and orange will develop in the copper under its transparent enamel covering. Fingers must be kept off the bare surface so skin oil does not prevent fusion between surface and enamel. Counterenamel should be applied before or after the formation of firescale on the surface.

Another method of utilizing copper scale is to apply opaque or transparent enamels freely over a bare copper surface, leaving certain areas free of enamel so scale can form on the exposed bare metal. The firescale surface can be left uncovered or it can be covered with more enamel in a transparent color. Although there are no set rules for designing with enamel and copper scale, bold and colorful designs are less apt to become lost against the dynamic firescale patterns.

COLOR PUDDLES. Gail Kristensen. A dynamic combination of bold pattern and firescale texture. Courtesy of the artist. *Photo by Kristensen.*

Small panel with firescale completely covered by fired flux enamel. It can be the base for an enamel painting.

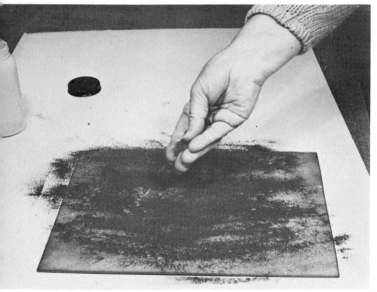

Black enamel is flung over a copper panel.

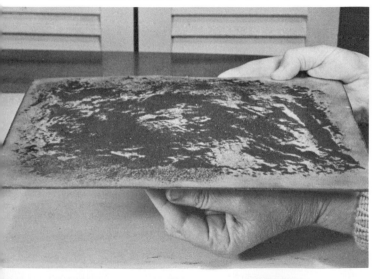

Sharp tapping from beneath makes little shock waves that move the enamel in rhythmic patterns.

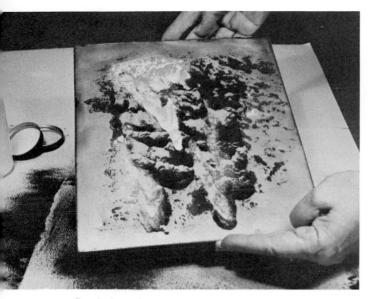 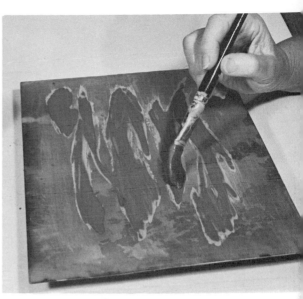

Small handfuls of white and gray opaque are dropped on the black pattern. The panel is rolled and tipped. The results can be fired for a very exciting effect.

Black 80-mesh enamel is ground finer in a mortar and pestle and is stirred into thin liquid flux. It is applied with a wide watercolor brush over a panel with a firescale base.

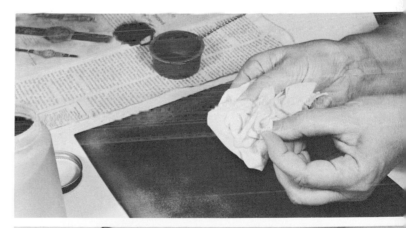

Flux is fired to both sides of a large panel. Black enamel is sifted over a wet, gummed surface. A piece of paper toweling is bunched into folds.

The paper is tamped on the *moist* black enamel for texture.

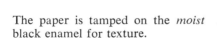

Large mural. Paul Hultberg. Copper scale across the base of the mural. Courtesy of the artist.

MURALS AND PANELS

The word "mural" is a French word meaning "applied to, or related to, a wall." The first prehistoric craftsman who frayed the end of a reed and used it to draw pictographs on his cave wall made his shelter more decorative, and his life safer from unknown forces, with murals. For ensuing thousands of years after the idea of wall decoration first took form and developed, basic themes remained close to their original concepts.

Gifted though he might be, the artist-craftsman could not give free reign to his dreamings. Strict traditional injunctions were assigned to wall decorations, especially to tomb drawings whose symbolic evocations sped the deceased on his transcendental journey. However proscribed those directives were, artists usually managed to show some originality in portraying basic themes.

In differentiating between murals and wall paintings, historians seem to indicate that early murals told a story or illustrated a theme, however veiled or obscure the theme may have been. Muslim wall paintings, for example, were never called murals. Muslim art was governed by religion. Strictures against any kind of imagery excluded nearly all images of man. Mosque walls were often completely covered with variations of the vine arabesque, but they were not referred to as murals.

In our time, murals are designed in many materials and sizes, and with complete freedom from restrictive rules. They may be constructed in one piece, in geometric panels, or in segments assembled as mosaics. This latter method is especially suitable for the craftsman whose kiln space limits the size of pieces he may fire.

Before copper is cut into small shapes, a scale drawing or plan is prepared so that

This careful artist works from a scale drawing to plan and cut copper (18-gauge) for her multilevel murals. Gail Kristensen cuts heavy copper with an electrical saw.

Each section of the mural is counterenameled and completed before she assembles the whole.

junctures form logical lines in the composition. Make cuts as clean as possible so that very little filing is necessary if you want a close fit between pieces. The most economical procedure is to cut pieces from one sheet of metal. If shapes are cut from several small metal pieces, be sure the pieces are of *identical gauge in thickness*.

Copper for murals that will be mounted flat against the background can be of thinner gauge than copper that will be mounted on planes set out from the wall or background panel. A good workable thickness is 20- or 22-gauge. Copper foil in 36-gauge is practical only when it is hammered or worked in some way to strengthen it. Even thicker gauges may be improved by working or beating, to take away the mill-rolled-sheet look. Keep panels flat by applying an equal thickness of enamel to each side. This can be done by adding flux to equalize thickness. Warpage will be toward the side of thinnest coverage.

When the mural is a large one, it is advisable to make a scale model first so that

PEACE. Pauli Lame. In its pristine simplicity, this mural has a message. The three-level panels are red, white, and blue, guarded by bristling brass rods. Courtesy of the artist.

problems are solved before actual construction of the large one begins. There are no
established procedures for designing or con-
structing a mural. Any method that works
for the individual craftsman is the logical
one to use.

Today's muralists are not content with
just dusting, dipping, and wet-packing; they
employ inventiveness and independence as
they survey their enamel "pigments" and
metal. Enamel is tossed or sifted over a copper base. It is brushed, rolled, tapped, or
manipulated in any manner to express an
idea, thought, or experience. This does not
mean that classical themes are abandoned
entirely. But they are developed in new ways.

Mural craftsmen ingeniously incorpo-
rate firescale into their palette of colors. They
may apply the torch and curl metal edges up
and over their enameled shapes. They can-
didly revel in the vibrancy of metal and
silicates, united by heat to produce exotic
color.

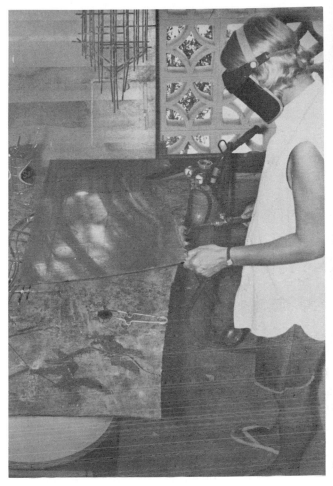

Pauli Lame works on a copper panel with an
acetylene and oxygen torch. Her work is mainly
large sculptural wall reliefs of brazed copper
shapes, attached to a welded brass framework.

MURAL PROJECT

A scale drawing is made to size, and tentative
colors are crayoned over the sketch.

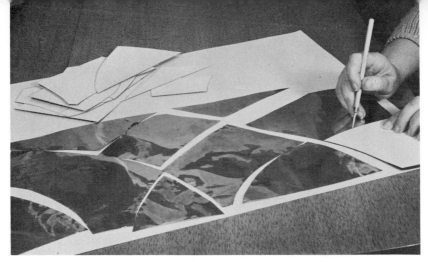

The drawing has been traced onto cardboard, which is cut out, and shapes are scored onto the copper with a scriber. The metal shapes are carefully cut out with metal shears.

Copper pieces are cleaned and painted on the underside with liquid flux for counterenamel.

Colors are sifted and trailed to approximate colors in the paper sketch.

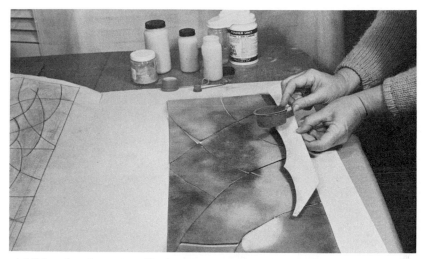

Additional colors are sifted over a cardboard outline stencil for soft defining edges. Notice that copper pieces are laid closely together.

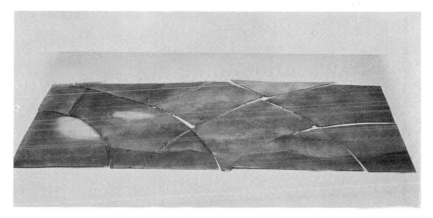

Both sides of the metal shapes were fired in one firing.

Details are added with black overglaze fine lines.

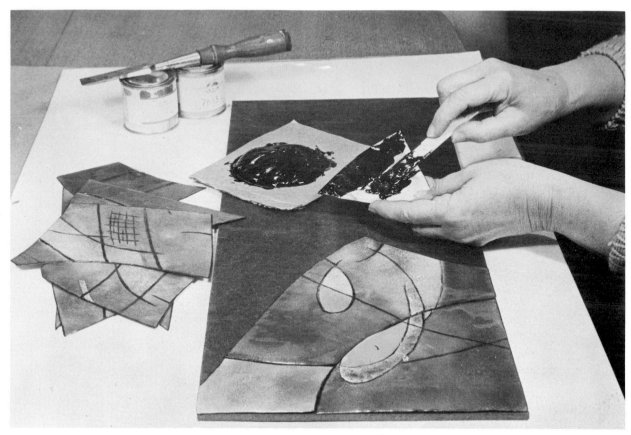

Two-component epoxy cement is mixed and applied to the back of each enameled shape. When all are pressed against the board, they are carefully aligned.

Scale model of a mural for a small chapel. Head scarf and cross are of silver foil covered in wet inlay. Lines where the pieces join are part of the design.

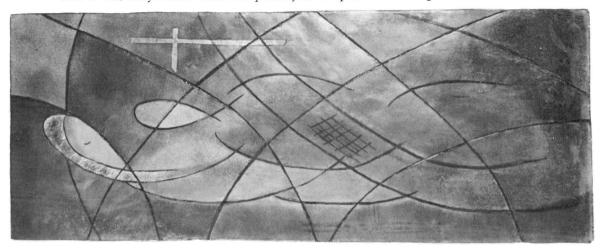

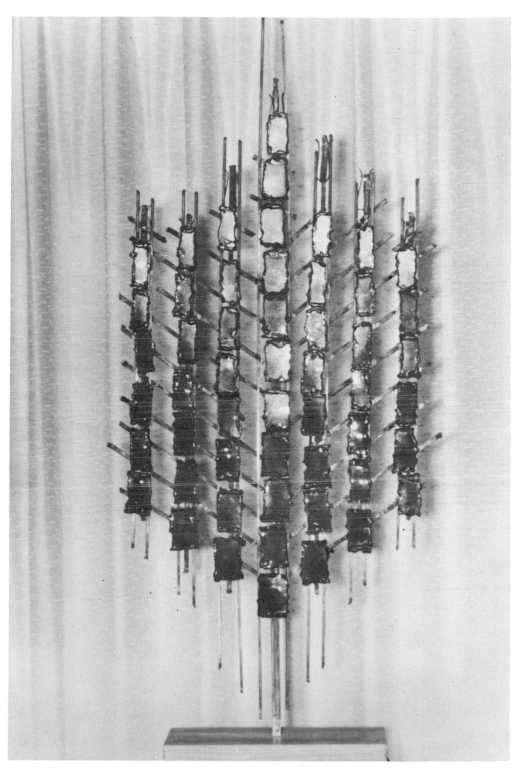

MENORAH. Pauli Lame. Candleholder. Metal edges of the enameled pieces receive a final melting in which the metal runs down and becomes copper luster. Courtesy of the artist.

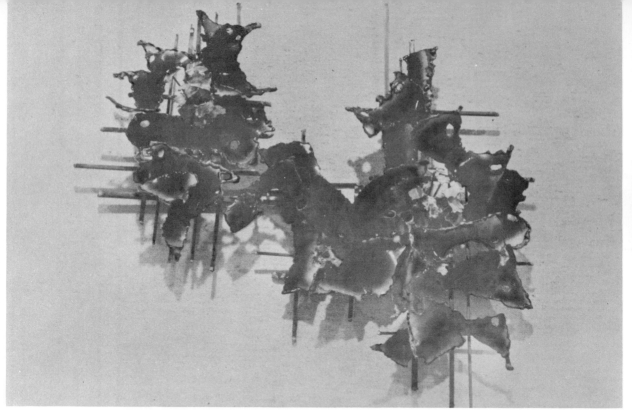

MARIPOSA-AZULES Y COSAS. Pauli Lame.
In her continuing experimentation, Pauli
Lame has developed a pierced metal and
luster effect that contrasts with the gem-
like character of transparent enamels.
Courtesy of the artist.

Large enameled mural. Paul Hultberg.
Liquid enamel with a wide band of oxidized copper across the panel. Courtesy
of the artist.

HIGH-FIRING TECHNIQUES

Separation Enamel

Separation enamel is a black oil-base liquid that produces an interesting pattern when it is fired over two or more colors that have been fired over a base coat of prefired flux. The patterns can be developed to show off the transparent depth of enamels. Like any other technique, whether or not it is excellent depends on the manner of its treatment.

There are two ways of using separation enamel. One method, used on flat surfaces, depends on the material's tendency to roll back the top layers of fired enamel to expose the base coat of flux. The longer the piece fires, the wider the pattern lines grow. The black separation enamel burns almost completely away, but sometimes it leaves fascinating flecks of black where it has not entirely disappeared. These black traces can be accentuated or extended with overglaze for a final firing. For this method, fire at about 1550° F. for about four minutes.

The other method is to brush simple patterns of black separation enamel around the top of a steep-sided piece, over prefired coats of enamel. Fire at about 1700° F. The separation enamel will roll back the top layers of enamel, at the same time flowing down the sides of the piece. This hot temperature consumes the black separation enamel completely.

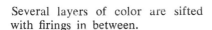

Several layers of color are sifted with firings in between.

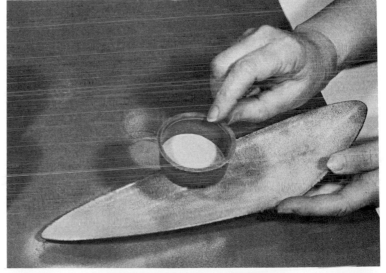

A free line design is brushed with separation enamel. It is dried ready for firing.

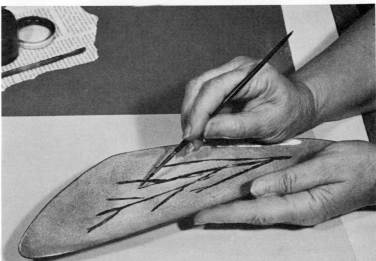

Overfiring (high-firing)

Firing enamels at hotter than the usually recommended temperatures can sometimes produce fascinating organic patterns. If the application of the colors is planned to create a definite effect, the process becomes controlled design rather than happenstance. The high-fired enamel will flow downward on an inclined surface. Fire a coat of liquid flux on the reverse side. On the side that will be designed, fire a coat of soft flux. Apply harmonizing colors (either opaque or transparent) one below the other, or side by side. Some white and black will sharpen the design. Before firing the piece, apply medium-fusing flux along the top edges to protect them from burning out.

The firing temperature is a most important factor. The piece must fire at 1700° F. for about three minutes. This requires the kiln temperature to be at least 1800° F. when the door is opened; it will drop somewhat at that time. The high-firing process depends on temperature control to produce the most exciting effects. The length of firing time must be controlled, too. It will not work to substitute a longer time for a high temperature. If a piece is fired for too long a time at too low a temperature, it will just burn away enamels, and the true beauty of "overfiring" will be missed.

Although separation enamel and "overfiring" are not new, they are not traditional techniques. There is still opportunity for considerable experimentation, especially in the area of controlling the results.

Tray was fired to 1550° F. or 1600° F. for about three minutes.

For a wider pattern, fire longer, about four minutes. It is advisable to watch from time to time so the piece can be removed when the rollback has reached the desired effect. Notice that lump enamel is fired with the lines. Interesting black flecks were emphasized.

An overfired bowl. Lillian Skaggs. Enamels were normal siftings of cardinal red opaque, fired with white. Mallard-blue transparent was sifted over all and fired quickly at 1700° F. for overfired texture. Courtesy of the artist.

Raised bowl, high-fired. For predictable effects, colors are carefully planned. Soft-fusing flux is fired over the exterior, liquid flux interior, with heavier siftings on the rim to guard against burned edges. Royal-blue opaque is fired over flux at normal temperature. Heavy siftings of opaque white were applied around the top, with narrow bands of green and black. The bowl was fired *right side up* at *1700° F.* for a few minutes.

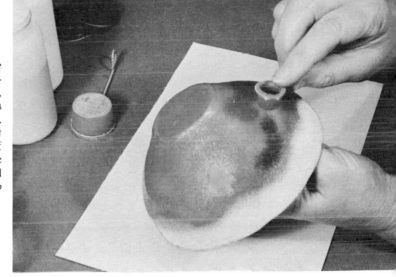

A band of dark transparent blue was fired above where the white had "slipped down." The bowl was fired *upside down* at 1500° F.

Textured panel. Catherine Munter. After continued experimentation, Catherine Munter developed a textured surface on enameled copper. She adds chemicals to the metal's surface in her development of firescale. When enamels are applied, they are treated with additives to give unusual textures and colorations. Courtesy of the artist.

Textured box lid #2. Catherine Munter. Courtesy of the artist.

ENAMELED METAL AND WOOD
APPLIQUÉ

When the enamelist goes far afield from the historical concept of enamels as embellishment for finely wrought metal objects, a logical step is away from metal itself as the most important area in a composition. Small pieces of enameled copper can be used in a variety of ways against panels built from woods applied in layers of unusual shapes.

Woods in several grains and colors, combined together, build a more exciting design than a composition all in one color or one wood. When you select the background wood panel, keep in mind the colors of the wood pieces that will be applied against it. Perhaps they may all have a reddish-brown color, for example cherrywood and mahogany. Yellow maple might be applied against a fruitwood finish. Some of the new metallic rubbing colors, wiped over the wood lightly, give an unusual effect.

If areas of wood and enameled metal are too equally balanced, the two materials will compete for attention and confuse the viewer. The composition is more effective when one or the other predominates. It may be a challenge at first for an enamelist to subordinate the enameled copper to the wood. But the true experimentalist will plunge right ahead and try different combinations of enameled metal and wood. Some interesting effects can be worked out with old weathered wood or driftwood.

If the pieces of enameled copper are slender or pointed, they may have a distressing tendency to curl up at the ends when they are enameled and fired on the first side. A simple way to prevent this is to enamel both sides and fire them in one firing. Paint liquid flux on the underneath surfaces and let it dry. Before the pieces are fired, spray the tops with gum and apply a generous coat of sifted enamel. Dry and fire both sides in one firing, at 1450° F. Take care not to disturb the dry liquid flux when the top surface enamel is applied. Designs are applied and given a second firing.

Each wood shape is roughened with an abrasive stone on the underneath surface; then it is cemented into place on the large background panel, and left to dry overnight. Enameled copper pieces are epoxied to the wood.

A panel of natural mahogany is rubbed with walnut varnish stain, which is quickly rubbed off so that only the heavy open pores are filled with darker color. Cardboard shapes are tried in various places to find the right composition.

The stylized bird form is traced on walnut. "Mountain" shapes are of cherry and walnut.

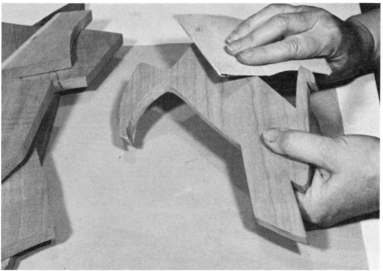

All wood pieces are cut on a band saw and smoothed with sandpaper.

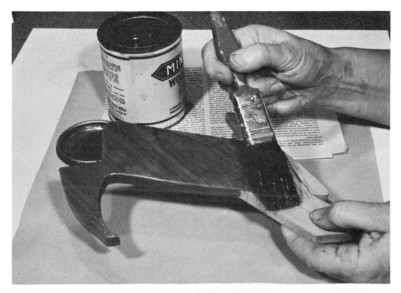

The wooden shapes are coated with natural Min-Wax, a combination wax and sealer. When it is dry, the natural wood color is rubbed with a rag to bring out the wax sheen. No finish is applied to the underside, which must have a *rough surface* for good cement adhesion.

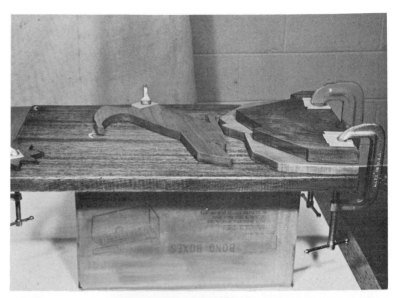

When all the pieces are finished, they are C-clamped together and left to dry overnight.

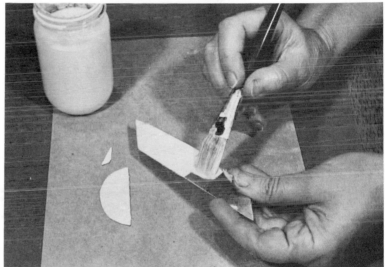

Small copper pieces are coated with liquid flux on the backs and left to dry.

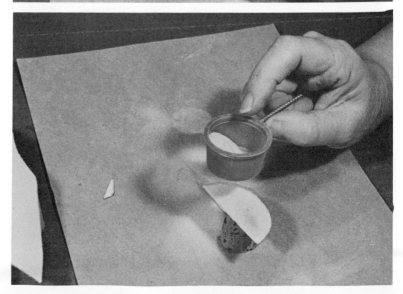

The fronts are dusted with colors, dried, and the pieces are fired. Black Jet Line accents are added and fired.

SUN WORSHIPER. Enameled pieces are cemented with epoxy glue.

SPRINGTIME. Polly Rothenberg. Rubbed mahogany panel, cherry-wood shapes, enameled copper wing shapes.

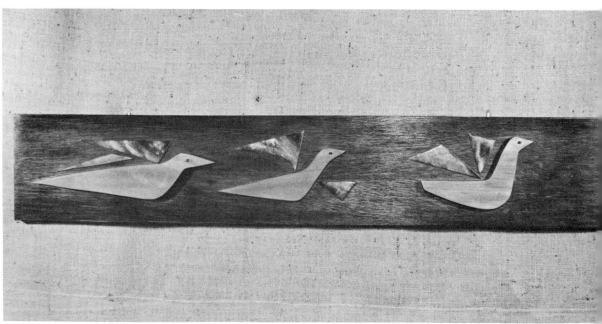

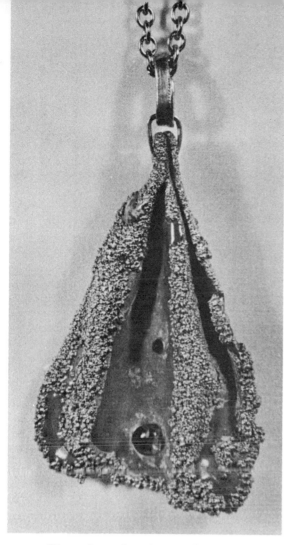

Electroformed and enameled pendant. Polly Rothenberg.

ENAMEL AND ELECTROFORMED COPPER

Electroplating is the electrochemical process of coating an article with a thin skin of metal or mixture of metals. The process of electrodeposition is not new to artists. Several groups of metalworkers over the country are now experimenting on new ways for the artist-craftsman to use this industrial process.

In *electroforming* as the enamelist uses it, the metal deposits are not closely controlled as in plating; the formations of metal particles are allowed to build up into bumpy and craggy nodules, much prized by the creative craftsman.

Basically, electrodeposition requires a source of direct current and an electrolyte bath, or solution. The direct current passes between a positive electrode, the anode, and a negative electrode, the cathode. The material to be plated is attached to the negative electrode; the material supplying the metal (copper, and so on) is attached to the positive electrode. The copper pieces can be suspended in the solution on copper or steel wires.

A factor of importance is the current density. When the current passes between the two electrodes in the bath, it distributes itself according to the path open to it. Thus very little current will reach the side of the object turned away from the anode bar. For more even distribution of copper particles, broad surfaces of the anode bar and the object receiving deposition should face one another, with the important side of the object facing the anode bar.

If there are deep hollows in the receiving piece, the current density in the depressions will be lower than on the raised portions, and the deposition of particles will be greater on the raised surfaces, projections, and corners of the pieces. If the object receiving the copper deposition is three-dimensional, a section of copper sheet can be bent to form a cylindrical anode bar that can be dropped around the art object in the electrolytic bath; or several smaller anode bars can be strung together inside the eletroforming tank, all connected by a copper wire to the positive anode. *For best results,* the electrolyte solution should be agitated (any kind of stirring device) and have a temperature of 70°–80° F. The copper should be chemically clean. The tank can be of glass, plastic, or ceramic crockery.

This basic description should be adequate to get interested enamel craftsmen started on experimenting with enamel and electroformed copper. (See illustrations.)

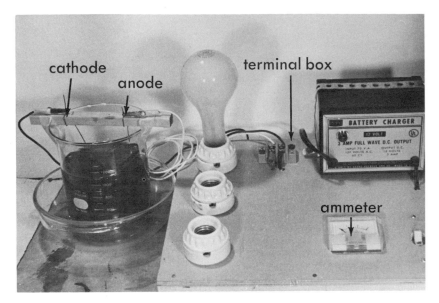

The Kreyes' electroforming equipment. The wire from the negative pole (cathode) of the battery charger goes to the copper object receiving deposition in the electrolyte tank, by way of a negative terminal box connection. This makes it easy to disconnect wires when the equipment is moved. The wire from the positive pole of the battery charger (anode) goes through the ammeter, through three #2 photoflood bulbs wired in parallel (instead of a rheostat) through the positive pole of the terminal box and then to the anode bar in the electrolyte bath.

Small copper spring jaws clamp the wires to the anode bar and the receiving object. The piece is checked for rate of deposition. Notice how the anode bar has been eaten away along the sides.

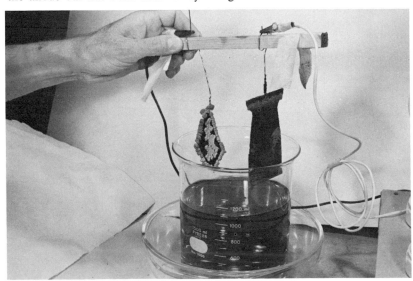

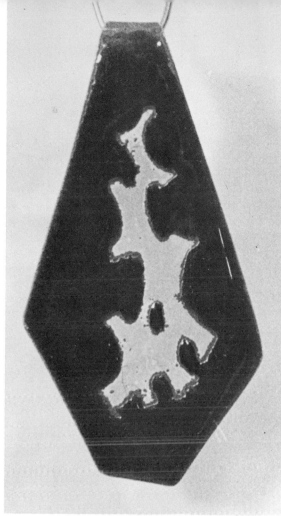

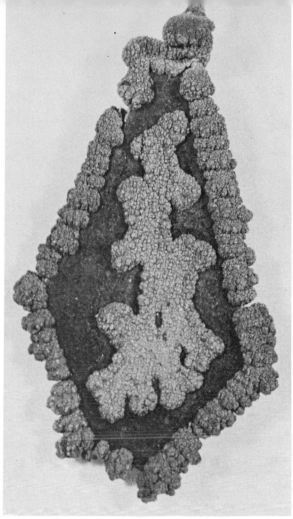

The demonstration piece before deposition. Bare copper stencil pattern and bare edges will receive the copper deposits.

After deposition, corners have extra buildup from three amperes of current. The piece may be fired to secure the deposition where it extends over the enamel.

Electroetching

For the artist, electroforming and electroetching are areas for exciting experimentation. Granular accumulations and etched organic depressions are perfect foils for the smooth, vibrant colors of enamels. There is still much to be discovered about the processes.

In electroetching, areas which are *not* to be cut away are stopped out with asphaltum varnish that is allowed to dry. The copper object to be *etched* is attached to the anode, or positive electrode, of the direct-current source (the battery charger). A piece of copper, which will *receive* the accumulation of particles etched away from the object, is attached to the negative electrode, or cathode. Thus the copper art object has changed places with the copper bar used as an anode bar in electroforming. Attach them with copper wire covered by wax.

To achieve a good etch, it is necessary to agitate and heat the solution to approximately 70° F. The electrolytic bath is the same solution used for electroforming.* Small accumulations of gases may occasionally collect on one or both electrodes. They will increase resistance and slow the copper deposition or etching. This occur-

---

* Do not use an aquarium tank for holding the electrolytic bath. The tar cement would contaminate the solution!

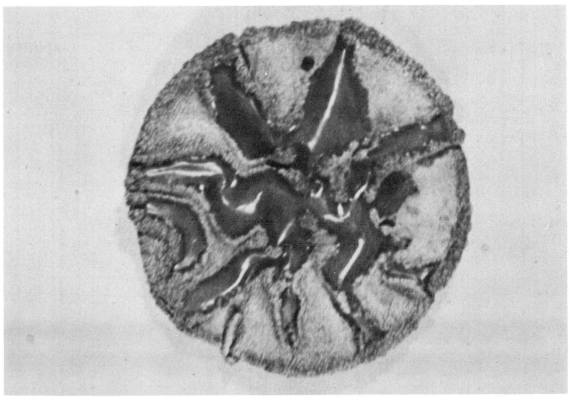

Box lids. Audrea Kreye. The square top was stopped out with asphaltum varnish in the depressions, then electroformed, cleaned, and enameled in wet inlay. The round lid was *enameled,* pickled, then electroformed, cleaned, and polished with a brass brush.

rence is called *polarization*. If this polarization is taking place, the amperage will drop perceptibly on the ammeter. Remove from the tank the copper pieces receiving and supplying copper particles and spray them with distilled water, then return them to the tank. Strain the electrolyte solution occasionally to remove accumulations of sediment. When the etching seems deep enough, the pieces are removed from the tank, and washed. If some areas are to be built up by electroforming, stop out etched areas with asphaltum varnish, let it dry, then switch positions of the pieces on the electrode wires and proceed with electroforming the piece. When the deposits have built up to the desired form, remove the copper object from the tank and clean it, ready for enameling. Snip off the wire.

These discussions of electroetching and electroforming are not intended as scientific presentations, but rather as a workable basis for further experimentation.

Warren Kreye and his wife, Audrea, of Ohio, combine their separate talents for electroforming and enameling copper. Warren Kreye's simple and inexpensive equipment begins with a battery charger (plugged into household outlet) for his source of direct current. The electrolyte solution used by the Kreyes for *copper* deposition is composed of copper sulfate, completely dissolved in distilled water, *to which* they add chemically pure concentrated sulfuric acid (water is never added *to* acid).

Proportions are:
Sulfuric acid (concentrated) 40cc/liter
(H_2SO_4)
Copper sulfate 250gm/liter
($CU SO_4 5H_2O$)

Audrea Kreye anneals the copper anode bar and pickles it; then she pickles the article to be plated, and rinses it. The use of three #2 photoflood bulbs in place of a rheostat in Warren's equipment makes a simple and less expensive method of controlling amperage of the current. For his particular solution and battery charger, one, two, and three light bulbs yield approximately one, two, and three amps respectively. Electroforming with one bulb gives a smooth deposit on the copper object, while three bulbs give a coarse deposit, which is more texturally interesting. One bulb used for two hours produces a fine-grained deposit on which to build the coarser grains. By switching from three or two back to one, a fine-grained deposit will cover and bind the coarse grains together. The time required is variable, but several hours are required for the complete process, even though Mrs. Kreye's pieces are small in size.

There are other metals that can be electroformed, but they require entirely different solutions. That used for silver is quite lethal, and should not be experimented with lightly. However, coordinated industrial arts and chemistry classes could utilize the Kreyes' ideas for inexpensive, yet imaginative and challenging projects in copper.

June Schwarcz of California, known internationally for her beautiful basse-taille enamels, combines electroforming with the etching of enameled copper bowls and panels. She etches, stops out areas with a resist such as asphaltum varnish, and then electroforms to give deeper relief; then she combines them with enamels. She masks designs on hammered bowls, leaving the top edge unprotected. The deposits build up around the edge of the bowl for an exciting contrast with the enameled interior.

Copper foil of about 36-gauge can be manipulated into folds and pleats on bowls. Mrs. Schwarcz forms it into pieces that would be impossible to shape with the heavier gauges of copper. Then she plates to give strength and character to the bowls that will be enameled. She makes very intricate surfaces by continually masking, etching, and depositing. This all fits in with her fondness for basse-taille work and its light-catching qualities that break up the surface plane, while magnifying and reflecting surface variations. June Schwarcz pioneered the technique of enameling electroformed copper.

June Schwarcz demonstrates one of her decorating processes. The bowl's interior is painted with asphaltum varnish; lines are scratched through the varnish. The bowl is put through the electrolyte bath and electroformed until the lines receive a deposit the thickness of a wire. The lines are pulled loose from their backing.

The exterior design is protected with asphaltum varnish. More lines are drawn on the interior surface, and broad areas are scratched through the varnish. The piece may either be returned to the electroforming tank for added deposition or it may be put into acid for etching as described under "Champlevé."

After removing the asphaltum varnish, the bowl is cleaned and polished, ready for enameling. Notice the copper lines broken loose earlier lying on the table in front of the bowl.

The bowl's exterior is not enameled. The interior is enameled; then the electroformed lines are fused into the enamel; *Photo by Bob Harwayne*. (This series of four photographs by courtesy of *Craft Horizons*.)

WOOD FORM. June Schwarcz. Etched copper with certain areas masked out and built higher, then enameled. Collection of Mr. and Mrs. Victor Honig, San Francisco.

FOREST II. June Schwarcz. Etched enameled copper mounted on marble slab. Collection of Dr. Irving R. Berlin, Seattle.

Box lid panel. Audrea and Warren Kreye. Asphaltum varnish was trailed in a design on 16-gauge copper. Back and edges of the panel were painted with the asphaltum. When it was dry, the panel was electroetched for a deep cut. The panel was cleaned, and black opaque enamel was applied in a champlevé design. Silver foil paillons were applied and covered with transparent old silver-gray. Enamel was stoned and waxed. Courtesy of the artists.

Basse-taille box lid. Audrea Kreye. A 20-gauge copper disk was sawed out with a ragged edge, then domed, annealed, and cleaned. Wire was attached for suspending disk in electrolytic bath. Asphaltum varnish was painted over V-patterns and border, and over edges and back of the disk. The parts left bare were *electroetched*. Next, the asphaltum varnish was cleaned with turpentine; the reverse areas were painted with the varnish, and the piece was returned to the bath for *electroforming* (the copper pieces changed places on the electrodes) to make the attractive nodular border. Asphaltum was cleaned off and the piece was filed to fit closely against the lid surface of the box it was designed to cover. The undersurface was painted with liquid flux and dried; the entire top center area was wet-packed with transparent gold enamel, dried, and fired at 1450° F. When cool, the nodular edge was scrubbed with Sparex solution, rinsed, and polished with a wire brush attached to a motor spindle. This lid is an excellent example of combination electroetch, electroform, and enamel. Courtesy of the artist.

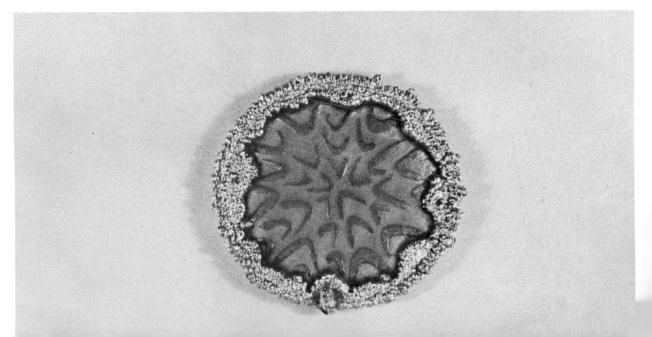

Additional Processes

FOOTED BOWLS

Forming the Foot

The selection of just the right foot for an enamel shape involves function as well as design. It is important to plan a foot which will complement the bowl's shape and also support the piece so that it will not topple over when it is put to use.

A metal spinner can form a foot for almost any shape; however, the facilities required for this work are not available to many craftsmen. An experienced metalsmith can form a foot from flat sheet copper, bend it to shape, and solder it together. The average enamelist in pursuit of low foot shapes can find pure copper pipe and tubing at his neighborhood plumbing contractor's shop. Copper "waste pipe" comes in sizes up to four inches in diameter. Short discarded

lengths are the easiest to handle and are the ones a contractor will often sell by the pound as scrap metal. Copper pipe can be sliced with a saw and further shaped over a metal stake for a very attractive bowl foot. For easy cutting, a #30 coping saw blade (30 teeth to the inch), with crimped or pegged ends snipped off, can be fastened into a jeweler's saw frame. A regular pipe cutter is a very handy tool for an enamelist to own.

Various small bowl and cup shapes, when inverted, make fine tall or short *tapered* feet. They can be soldered into place just as they come, or the base can be cut off and only the rim part used. If the base is left on, anneal the pieces, then tap flat the bottom surface of each shape for a good juncture of the two forms. When the foot has been checked for an even fit, it is cleaned of grease and soil, ready for soldering.

White compote. Treva Runyon. This handsome piece needs no surface enrichment. The rim around the bowl and foot is 9-gauge copper wire. The
knob is copper tubing and a slice of copper pipe. Enameled entirely in spot-
less white opaque. Courtesy of the artist. *Photo by Audio Visual Service of
Miami.*

Various copper shapes suitable for forming bowl and rim feet.

Pipe is sawed with a jeweler's saw for a low rim foot.

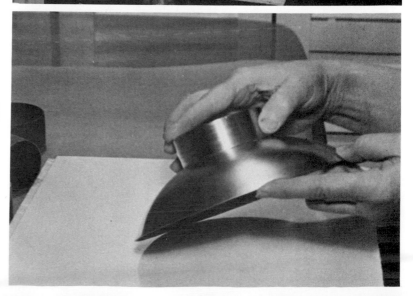

The foot must fit the contour of the bowl's base. It is filed and stoned until it fits perfectly.

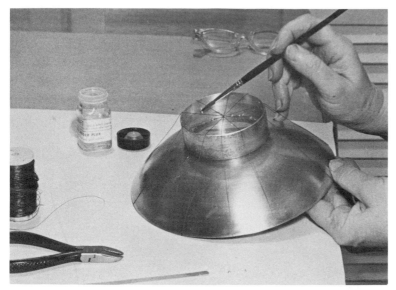

Binding wire around bowl and foot holds it securely. Pick up pieces of IT solder with flux-moistened brush, and place them all around the fluxed juncture between rim and bowl.

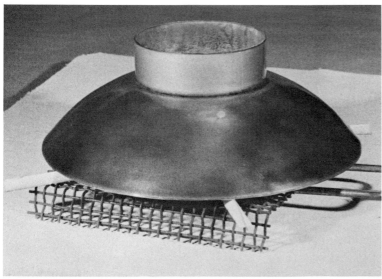

If any gaps appear between bowl and rim foot, pack them with moist enamel and refire, keeping temperature around 1400° F. to make sure the solder does not remelt.

Enamel is applied to the bowl's interior.

Soldering in the Kiln

When the bowl and foot are clean and dry, paint the areas that will be joined with liquid soldering flux for silver (it has no connection with flux enamel), then let it dry completely. Soldering flux will hold back oxidation of the metal, and the silver solder will follow the flux along the crack where bowl and foot join, when sufficient heat is applied. CAUTION—do not put flux where you do not want the solder to flow. Confine it to the juncture area. Wrap iron binding wire around bowl and foot to hold them in position.

Silver solder comes in round or flat wire form. It also has a variety of melting temperatures. For soldering together two copper pieces that will eventually be enameled, use the *hard* silver solder in flat ribbon form, with a flow point of 1425° F.; or, if it is available, the IT grade with a flow point of 1460° F. is even better. Firing temperature when the piece is enameled must be kept *below* the solder's flow point. (That is the only necessary precaution when enameling soldered pieces.) Clean the solder.

Cut the ribbon of solder with sharp scissors by fringing an end of the piece, then cut across the fringe. Make the pieces about 1/32 of an inch square. Pick up each piece of solder with a flux-moistened brush, and position them all along the crack between foot and bowl, *touching both foot and bowl.* Let the flux dry.

When copper is preheated for soldering, rapid oxidation is a problem. The copper pieces must be heated as quickly as possible. Metalsmiths often apply a torch for soldering, but it is fairly difficult to heat a large copper bowl and foot rapidly enough to prevent heavy oxidation. It is relatively simple to raise the kiln temperature to about 1700° F., then place the wire-bound foot and bowl, with solder in place, on a trivet and put them in the kiln on a firing rack. If the flux is not completely dry, steam will form and bits of solder will pop loose. They must be replaced or removed before firing continues. The temperature will drop when the door is opened. By leaving the door slightly ajar, you may control the heat to just above the solder's indicated flow point. It should be watched constantly. As soon as the solder melts, or "flows," remove the piece from the kiln and allow it to cool. Some practice may be required before you can easily recognize, by the silvery streak along the juncture, that the solder has flowed.

If the bowl is put into the kiln at a temperature below the solder's melting point, heavy firescale will form before the heat can be brought up to melting or flow point; this will prevent the solder from adhering to the copper, the cause for many failures.

When the soldered piece has cooled, remove the binding wire, and clean the piece as usual. Because the heat has also annealed the metal, it is rather soft and must be handled carefully. It is natural to grasp a bowl by the rim; but this can result in bent or wavy edges that often go unnoticed until the bowl has been enameled and it is too late to correct it.

Enameling the Soldered Piece

The inside of the foot area is easily enameled with liquid flux enamel. A light sifting of a color over it may be desired. It is important to use low-firing enamels on soldered pieces. Most transparents have lower fusing temperatures than opaques. Some opaques, such as ivory, beige, yellow, and a few others, are high-firing and are best bypassed on soldered pieces. The temperature *must* be kept near 1400° F. to prevent the solder from remelting and loosening. With patience and meticulous attention to important details, you may successfully accomplish a footed-shape project; the result will be a very handsome piece.

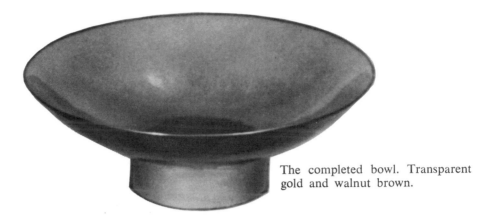

The completed bowl. Transparent gold and walnut brown.

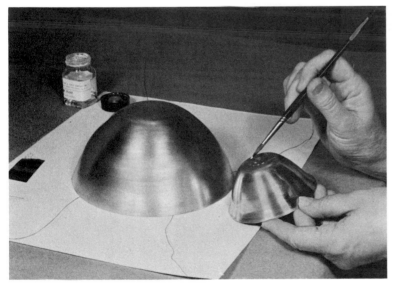

Binding wire is brought up and over the two shapes, and twisted to hold them securely in place while they are fired.

Footed bowl. Polly Rothenberg. The firescale pattern on this bowl was formed *before* the foot was attached, soldered, and enameled.

Green compote. Polly Rothenberg. Transparent gold interior, transparent emerald-green exterior. Collection of Mr. and Mrs. Edwin Oxner, San Jose, California.

Blue bowl. Polly Rothenberg. Soldered rim foot.

APPLICATION OF JEWELRY FINDINGS

The application of delicate findings to enameled jewelry presents special problems. Although aesthetically, silver solder is most appropriate on silver jewelry, if a temperature high enough to melt silver solder is applied to a piece of enameled jewelry, the enameled parts will crack. Delicate findings cannot be soldered before the enamel is fired. They will anneal and become soft and easily bent. There are soft lead-base solders that melt at very low temperatures and, if neatly applied, they prove quite satisfactory. In addition, there are two-component epoxy cements that are finding more and more favor with enamelers.

Earrings and Cuff Links

When earrings and cuff links are enameled, leave a small bare metal spot on the back of each piece to receive the finding. Clean it thoroughly so the solder will adhere. If low-fusing solder wire is used, touch the spot to which the finding will be attached *and* the inside of the earring cup with soft-solder flux. Moisten a small brush with the flux. Then use it to pick up the tiny particles of soft-solder wire (or strip) and put them into each earring cup or on the cuff-link finding pad, which will be soldered to a bare spot on the back of a piece. The finding is not positioned yet, but is held upside down and heated with a very gentle flame until the solder melts. Let it cool; then position the finding over the bare spot on the cuff-link or earring back. Make sure the finding is correctly aligned with the front. Again heat the piece, not the finding, until the solder *flows*. It will show as a glistening line around the contact point. Remove the flame and cool the piece. The solder will stay fluid for a while. *Overheating* will *break* down solder and flux to the point that they will not hold.

Self-fluxing solder that comes in a tube must be kneaded thoroughly to mix the solder and flux each time before the tube is opened. Put about three small pinheads of solder on each finding pad and set it into place on a bare metal spot. Play the flame gently *around* the solder area (not directly on it) just long enough for the solder to show as a bright line around the edge of the finding. Let it cool before it is moved. The crust of excess oxides and dried flux that collects should be removed with a fine abrasive cloth or a buffing wheel.

Pendants

A pendant loop can be very attractively included in the pendant's design and become an integral part of the whole piece. Or a small separate loop can be soldered into place on the pendant's back before the piece is enameled. IT hard silver solder (melting point, 1460° F.) is valuable for soldering pieces that will be enameled.

Flux the back of the pendant on the spot where the finding will be attached, but not beyond that spot or the surplus flux might cause the solder to flow beyond the designated area. Flux the loop and the solder. Put tiny pieces of solder on the loop contact point, and melt them. When the metal has cooled, set the loop on the pendant back (solder against pendant), and play the torch flame over the pendant to heat it enough to melt the solder. Remove the torch when the glistening flow line appears between loop and pendant.

The firing temperature for *enameling* the soldered pendant must not go higher than 1425° F. to guard against the solder remelting when the piece is fired. Pack moist enamel around the pendant loop. The main counterenamel surface area can be dusted or wet-packed.

Jewelry. Miriam Elsbree. Top to bottom: pin with tiny enamel fans in the wet-inlay method; silver earrings constructed of silver sheet; small round cloisonné pin; pendant with silver wire "cord." The pivot construction between front and back of the cord makes it comfortable to wear. Courtesy of the artist.

Paper frisket is placed on the spot where the finding will be soldered or cemented. The frisket must be removed before firing.

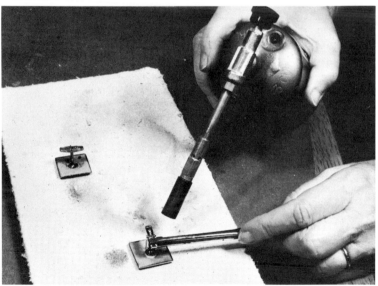

For soft solder on enameled pieces, a wide tip on the torch is less likely to overheat the enamel and crack it. Play the flame lightly and keep it moving around the solder, not on it.

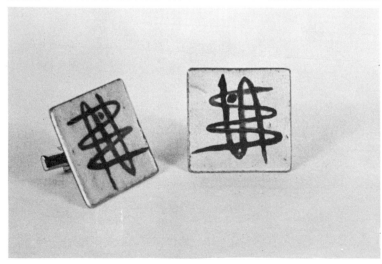

Cuff links are underglaze over bare copper with a covering coat of transparent enamel.

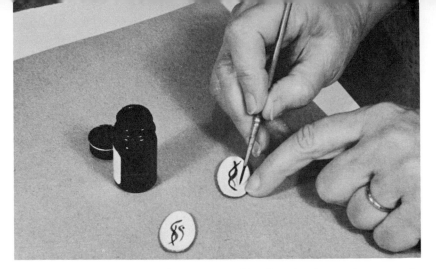

Designs on earrings and cuff links should "face" each other, or be *reversed*. Overglaze on white enamel.

Earrings were given a coat of green-gold transparent and a sifting of black. Findings are attached in the same way as for cuff links.

Small jewelry pieces are easily fired on nichrome wires stuck into soft insulating brick (not hard firebrick).

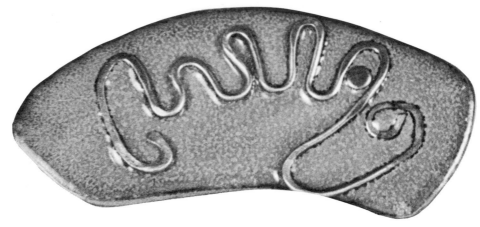

Pin with embedded silver wire.
Transparent turquoise is fired over
opaque light blue. The wire was
pounded.

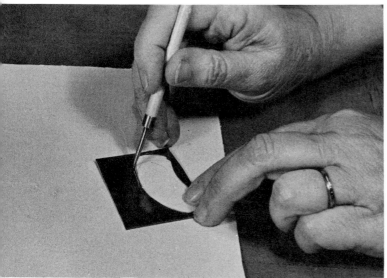

Scribe around a cardboard shape.
Cut out the pin with metal shears.

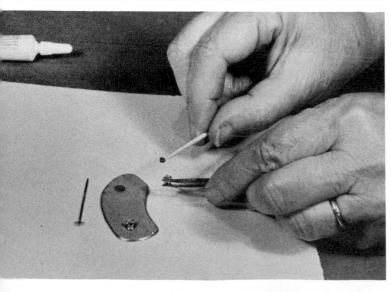

The pin is enameled on both sides
with spots left bare to receive the
pin findings. On *enameled* pieces,
very soft solder is applied to and
melted on each part separately. The
flow point of some soft solders is
as low as 300° F., and very little
heat is required to melt them.

Notice that pin parts are not aligned but are slightly offset to give tension to the pin when it is closed. Pin parts are applied *above* the center line. A safety catch should be half open when solder is applied. Keep solder out of the catch opening, or it may solder shut. Catch is to right of joint, with the opening facing down. Insert fixed rivets of the stem into the joint, and press the joint closed with jewelry pliers.

Pins

There are various kinds of pin findings available on the market. Because usually an enamel craftsman must apply delicate findings after the jewelry piece is enameled, except in the case of pendants, and must use very low-fusing solder, a special kind of pin catch and joint with a wide soft-soldering patch is advisable. This applies to findings with separate catch and pin stem joint. There are also combination pin backs that are most often used on copper jewelry. A bare metal spot must be left in the counterenamel to receive the pin findings, whether they will be soldered or cemented. For good adhesion, the spot should be scratched or roughened before the solder or the cement is applied. Apply the solder and finding as described for applying soft solder to earrings.

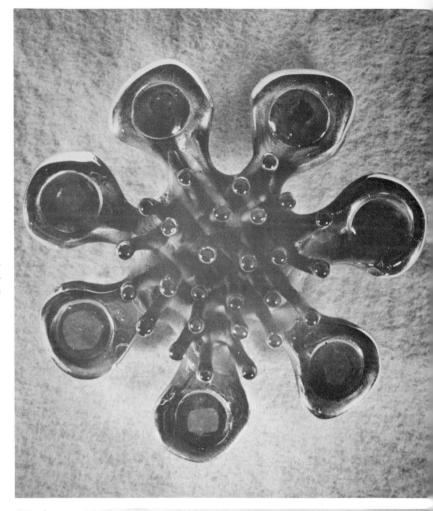

Cast silver pin. Audrey Engstrom. Plique-à-jour and enamel jewels. Courtesy of the
artist.

Cast gold ring. Rama Webb.
Blue enamel base and plique-
à-jour with pearl. Courtesy of
the artist.

Rings. Rama Webb. Left, turquoise cloisonné on a constructed ring. Right, cast gold ring with blue, red, and white opaques. Courtesy of the artist.

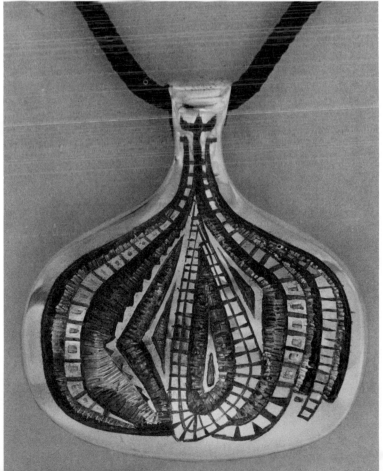

Engraved champlevé pendant. Harold Hasselschwert. The pendant loop is beautifully incorporated into the design of the piece. Courtesy of the artist.

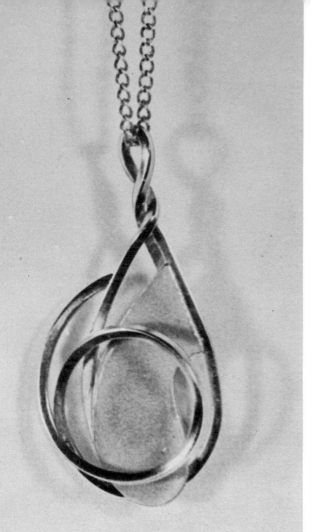

Fine silver pendant. Polly Rothenberg.
Constructed of square silver wire and
small silver panel soldered with IT silver
solder. Enamel is applied thinly in wet-
inlay process. Firing temperature is 1400°
F.

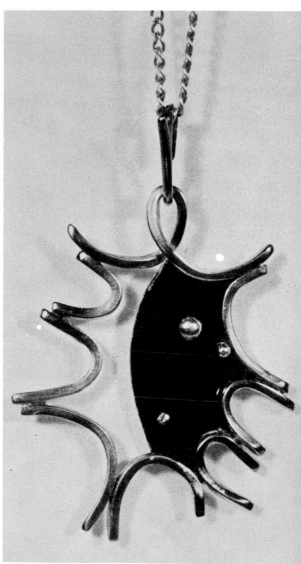

Fine silver pendant. Polly Rothenberg.
Forged wire, sheet, and silver balls are
soldered with hard silver solder. Black
opaque enamel is fired at 1350° F.

Perfume-bottle pendant. Audrey Engstrom. A delightful cloisonné fine-silver piece. Links are hand forged. Courtesy of the artist.

DANCING COUPLE. Brooch. Sigurd Alf Eriksen. Soldered frame with raised oval center. Enameled in bright opaque colors. Courtesy of the Cooper-Hewitt Museum, Smithsonian Institution.

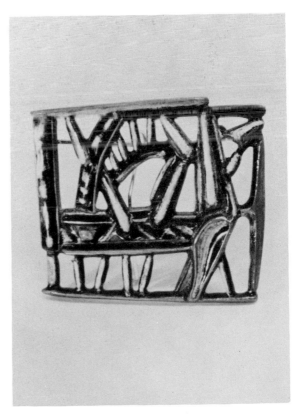

DEER. Brooch. Sigurd Alf Eriksen. Champlevé enamel on silver-gilt base. Enameled in black, white, and green. Courtesy of Cooper-Hewitt Museum, Smithsonian Institution.

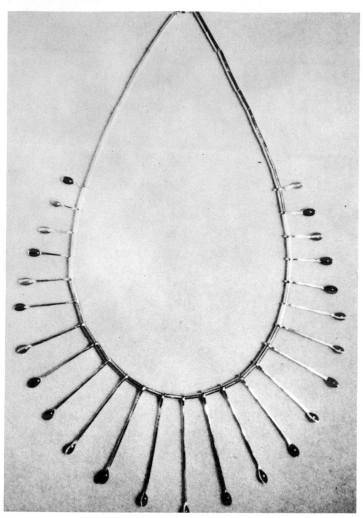

Necklace. Audrey Engstrom. Forged silver with enamel jewels. Courtesy of the artist. *Photo by Robert Engstrom.*

Necklace. Arline Fisch. Champlevé enamel on forged silver. Courtesy of the artist. *Photo by Lynn Fayman's Studio.*

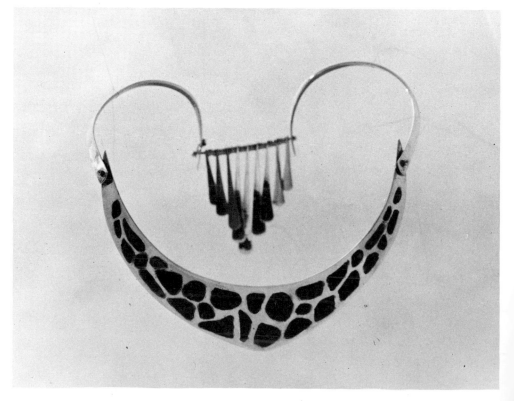

Bibliography

ALBERS, JOSEF. *American Abstract Artists*. New York: The Ram Press, 1946.

ALMEIDA, OSCAR. *Metalwork and Its Decoration by Etching*. London: Mills and Boon, Ltd., 1966.

AMACO. *Metal Enameling Handbook*. Indianapolis: The American Art Clay Co., Inc., 1968.

BAGER, BERTEL. *Nature as a Designer*. New York: Reinhold Publishing Corp., 1967.

BAINBRIDGE, HENRY CHARLES. *Peter Carl Fabergé*. London: Spring Books, 1966.

BATES, KENNETH F. *Enameling Principles and Practice*. Cleveland and New York: The World Publishing Co., 1951.

———. *The Enamelist*. Cleveland and New York: The World Publishing Co., 1967.

BIRREN, FABER. *Creative Color*. New York: Reinhold Publishing Corp., 1961.

BLUM, WILLIAM, and HOGABOOM, GEORGE. *Principles of Electroplating and Electroforming*, New York: McGraw-Hill Book Company, Inc., 1945.

BOVIN, MURRAY. *Silversmithing and Art Metal for Schools, Tradesmen, Craftsmen*. New York: Murray Bovin, 1963.

CHENEY, SHELDON. *A World History of Art*. New York: The Viking Press, Inc., 1937.

———. *The Story of Modern Art*. New York: The Viking Press, Inc., 1958.

CHOATE, SHARR. *Creative Casting*. New York: Crown Publishers, Inc., 1966.

CLARKE, GEOFFREY, and FEHER, FRANCIS and IDA. *The Technique of Enameling*. New York: Reinhold Publishing Corp., and London: B. T. Batsford, 1967.

DUTTON, NINETTE. *The Beautiful Art of Enameling*. New York: Arc Books, Inc., 1966.

Encyclopaedia Britannica. "Enameling Process." Volume VIII, pp. 353–357. 1967.

Encyclopedia Americana. "Enamels and Enameling." Volume X, pp. 311–313. 1963.

GOMBRICH, E. H. *The Story of Art*. London: Phaeden Press, and Garden City, New York: Doubleday and Company, Inc., 1960.

KINNEY, KAY. *Glass Craft*. Philadelphia: Chilton Books, 1962.

MEILACH, DONA, and SEIDEN, DONALD. *Direct Metal Sculpture*. New York: Crown Publishers, Inc., 1966.

NEWBLE, BRIAN. *Practical Enamelling and Jewelry Work*. New York: The Viking Press, Inc., and London: Studio Vista, 1967.

REBERT, JO, and O'HARA, JEAN. *Copper Enameling*. Columbus, Ohio: Professional Publications, Inc., 1956.

SHOENFELT, JOSEPH F. *Designing and Making Handwrought Jewelry*. New York: McGraw-Hill Book Co., Inc., 1960.

STRIBLING, MARY LOU. *Mosaic Techniques*. New York: Crown Publishers, Inc., 1966.

THOMPSON, THOMAS E. *Enameling on Copper and Other Metals*. Highland Park, Illinois: T. C. Thompson Company, 1950.

UNTRACHT, OPPI. *Enameling on Metal*. Philadelphia and New York: Chilton Books, 1962.

———. *Metal Techniques for Craftsmen*. Garden City, New York: Doubleday and Company, Inc., 1968.

VON NEUMANN, ROBERT. *The Design and Creation of Jewelry*. Philadelphia and New York: Chilton Books, 1963.

WEDD, J. A. DUNKIN. *Pattern and Texture*. New York and London: The Studio Publications, 1956.

WINTER, EDWARD. *Enamel Art on Metals*. New York: Watson-Guptil Publications, 1958.

PERIODICALS

Ceramics Monthly Magazine, Columbus, Ohio.

Craft Horizons. New York, New York.

Plating. Journal of the American Electroplaters' Society. Newark, New Jersey.

Glossary

(The glossary is intended for quick reference; consult index and text for detailed explanations.)

Abrasive: A substance used for grinding and polishing.

Acid: A pickling or etching compound or solution.

Acid Resist: Material, such as asphaltum varnish, painted on metal to resist acid in the etching process.

Adhesive Gums: Agar, arabic, or tragacanth gums that bind powdered enamels to a surface, and burn away in firing.

Aerosol: Compressed gas in a small container.

Agar: An adhesive enameling gum derived from seaweed.

Alloy: Different metals fused together and completely intermixed.

Anneal: To make metal malleable by subjecting it to high heat, then cooling it.

Anode: The positive pole of an electrolytic cell.

Anode Bar: Metal attached to the anode, in an electrolyte bath, which supplies the particles for electrodeposition.

Appliqué: Shapes applied to a surface to build up a layered design.

Asbestos Mittens: Heat-resistant mittens or gloves intended for handling hot objects.

Asphaltum Varnish: Black tar used as an acid resist in etching metal.

Atomizer: A device for reducing liquid adhesives to a fine spray.

Backing Enamel: Usually a mixture of odds and ends of 80-mesh enamels applied as a counterenamel to prevent warping.

Ball Peen Hammer: A metal hammer with one end of the head round and the other end flat.

Basse-Taille (low cut): A decorating technique where the metal surface is engraved, etched, gouged, or hammered, then completely covered with transparent enamels.

Bezel: A metal collar for securing objects such as gems and stones.

Binding Wire: Soft annealed fine iron wire for binding together parts being soldered.

Borax: A sodium borate ingredient combined with silicates in the manufacture of enamels.

Braze: To join metal to metal with torch, flux, and a metal rod having a lower melting point (but over 1000° F.) than the metals being joined.

Burnish: To smooth a metal surface with a rounded, highly polished hard metal tool.

Carborundum Stone: An abrasive stone.

Casting: Process of making metal forms by filling a hollow mold with molten metal.

Cathode: The negative pole of an electrolytic cell.

Champlevé: Design depressed in metal, then filled with enamels.

Charge: To fill a brush or to lay a brush-load on a surface.

Chase: To make depressions by hammering a tool against a metal surface.

Chasing Tool: The steel tool used for chasing.

Cloisonné: A decorative technique employing thin metal wire attached to a metal or enamel surface to define areas that may be filled with enamel colors.

Cloisons: Enclosures made of thin metal wires.

Concentric: Lines within lines, having a common center but not tangent to one another.

Contamination: Unwanted particles or impurities.

Counterenamel: Enamel fired on the back of a piece to equalize tensions.

Crackle Enamel: A decorative enamel that produces a pronounced crackled pattern when fired over an enamel undercoat.

Crawling: A slumping effect caused by excessive enamel or gum application.

Doming Block: A metal cube with rounded depressions for shaping jewelry.

Dusting: Applying fine enamel grains through a sieve.

Electroetch: To eat away metal by electrochemical process.

Electroform: To form shaped objects by electrodeposition of metal particles on a mold.

Electroplate: To coat with an even metal skin by electrodeposition.

Element (electrical): The coiled wires that provide heat in an electric kiln.

Emery Cloth: A cloth coated with fine-grained abrasive material, for smoothing and polishing metals.

Epoxy Cement: A two-component thermosetting resin glue that forms a strong bonding agent.

Etching: Eating away of metal.

Fanning: Slightly opening and closing kiln door to lower temperature.

Findings: Functional attachments for jewelry.

Fine Gold: Pure gold.

Fine Line (or *Jet Line*) *Black:* Trade names for dense black overglaze enamel in a liquid medium.

Fine Silver: Pure silver.

Firebrick: A dense brick capable of sustaining high temperatures, used for lining furnaces or kilns.

Firescale: Metal surface residue resulting from exposure to high temperature in the kiln.

Firing Fork: A long-handled two-pronged tool for lifting trivets and firing racks into and out of the kiln.

Flow Point: The temperature at which heated solder liquifies.

Flux 1: A colorless transparent enamel.
2: A substance for promoting fusion in soldering or brazing.

Foil: A tissue-thin sheet of metal.

Found Objects: Any objects, found anywhere, that may be adapted creatively to art or craft objects.

Frit: Enamel in coarse particles.

Gauge: A measurement to indicate thickness of metal.

Glaze: To coat with a glossy surface or glass coating.

Glaze Surfacer: A liquid applied to surfaces to retard oxidation of metals or to provide a glossy coating.

Graver: A tool for engraving metals.

Grisaille: Decorating enamel in white and gray values on a dark background.

Gum Tragacanth: An enameling adhesive derived from herbs.

Hot-Plate Kiln: A small hot plate with removable top, designed for enameling jewelry and small trays.

Inorganic: Not derived from vegetable or animal matter.

Iridescence: A rainbow-like play of colors responsive to changes in light and viewing angle.

Jewels: A term identifying lump enamels that form a rounded jewel shape after firing.

Jump Ring: A small metal ring that links together two metal loops.

K.: Abbreviation for "karat," used to identify purity of gold.

Kiln: A high-temperature furnace for firing enamels, glass, or clay.

Kiln Cement: Refractory cement for repairing walls and floors of kilns.

Kiln Shelf: A refractory slab placed at the bottom of the firing chamber or propped above it.

Kiln Wash: Flint and clay mixture for coating the floor or shelf of a kiln, to collect molten drippings.

Lavender Oil (see *Oil of Lavender*).

Lethal: Deadly.

Limoges: Enamel painting technique first introduced in Limoges, France, during the Renaissance.

Limpid: Marked by serene transparency; appearing to flow under the surface.

Liquid Flux: Finely ground, colorless transparent enamel in a liquid medium.

Liver of sulfur: A sulfur compound for darkening metal decoratively by giving it an oxidized or antique finish.

Low-Fire Enamel: Enamel that fuses at lower than 1400° F. temperature.

Luster (or *Lustre*): Fine metallic particles in a liquid medium, for decorating enameled pieces in gold or silver color by brush or pen.

Lustre Essence: Liquid for thinning or cleaning unfired lusters.

Malleable: Capable of being easily shaped; not brittle.

Mallet: A short-handled hammer with a large cylindrical head of wood, leather, or rubber.

Mesh: A measurement of particle sizes as they are sorted through the number of sieve openings in a square inch.

Metallic Oxides: Color ingredients in enamels, derived from metals.

Mica: A transparent mineral silicate not affected by heat, and readily separated into very thin sheets.

Monel Metal: A nickel-copper alloy that resists firescale formation.

Mortar and Pestle: An extremely hard vessel and club-shaped implement for grinding enamels.

Nichrome: An acid-resisting refractory alloy of nickel, iron, and chromium, not subject to firescale.

Nitric Acid: A corrosive acid that may be diluted into different strengths for pickling and etching.

Oil of Lavender: A volatile liquid vehicle for finely ground painting enamels.

Opalescent Enamels: Semitransparent enamels.

Opaque Enamels: Nontransparent enamels that cover and conceal the metal or enamel underneath.

Overfire: To fire at higher heat than normally recommended temperatures.

Overglaze: Finely ground enamels in a liquid medium for painting over fired enamels.

Oxidation: Discoloration of metal by exposure to heat air, or chemical.

Paillons: Thin pieces of metallic foils.

Pickling: Subjecting metal to an acid bath to soften and remove discoloration and soil.

Planishing: Final light hammering to smooth out a metal surface.

Plique-à-Jour: Transparent enamels fired into openings in metal.

Pyrometer: An instrument for measuring and indicating temperature, especially in a kiln.

Refractory: Capable of sustaining high temperatures.

Repoussé: Design on metal made by hammering the reverse side, as well as chasing on the top surface.

Resist (see *Acid Resist*).

Rheostat: A device for regulating electric current.

Scale Inhibitor: A liquid compound painted on bare metal to control firescale formation in the kiln.

Scriber: A pointed tool for scratching lines on metal.

Scrolling: Creating designs by pulling a pointed and angled tool through molten enamel in the kiln.

Sgraffito: The technique of scratching through a layer of unfired enamel to reveal the enamel or metal underneath.

Shellac Mounting Stick: A wooden handle attached to wood disk on which shellac is melted; used for holding small metal pieces to be engraved.

Sifting: Dusting dry granular enamels through a mesh.

Spun Shapes: Metal bowls formed by spinning sheet metal disks on a lathe.

Stake: A metal tool with one rounded end for forming metal shapes.

Star Stilts: Three- or four-pointed steel-tipped ceramic stilts for supporting pieces in the kiln.

Starting Block: A hardwood block with shallow saucer-shaped depressions for shaping metals.

Sterling Silver: 92.5 percent pure silver and 7.5 percent alloy.

Stoning: Grinding with a fine carborundum stone under running water.

Tangent: Touching but not crossing.

Texture: Surface structure of roughness and smoothness.

Thermosetting: The property of becoming permanently rigid when cured or heated slightly.

Toxic: Poisonous.

Transite: A hard heatproof composition board.

Translucent: Between transparent and opaque.

Transparent Enamels: Enamels having the property of transmitting light and refractions of light from enamels or metal underneath.

Trivet: A pronged metal support for holding an enameled piece in the kiln.

Undercoat: A fired coat of enamel over which one or more additional layers of enamel will be fired.

Underfire: To subject to too low a temperature or for too short a time in the kiln.

Underglaze: Painted opaque enamel over which transparent enamel is to be fired.

Value: Quality of lightness or darkness of colors.

Vise: A device having two movable jaws for firmly holding objects being worked on (usually fastened to the edge of a bench or table).

Vitreous Enamel: Silicate compounds for fusing to metals by firing.

Warping: Distortion of metal usually caused by heat plus uneven stresses.

Wet-Pack to (also *to wet inlay* and *to wet charge*)*:* To lay on moist enamels by packing with small tools.

Supply Sources

UNITED STATES

Enamels and Supplies

American Art Clay Co.
4717 W. 16th Street
Indianapolis, Indiana 46222

Norbert L. Cochran
2540 S. Fletcher Avenue
Fernandina Beach, Florida 32034

Thomas C. Thompson Co.
1539 Old Deerfield Road
Highland Park, Illinois 60035

Enameling Supplies, General

Arts and Crafts Colony
4132 N. Tamiami Trail
Sarasota, Florida 33580

Bergen Arts and Crafts
Box 689
Salem, Massachusetts 01971

Illini Ceramic Service
439 N. Wells
Chicago, Illinois 60610

Immerman Crafts, Inc.
16912 Miles Avenue
Cleveland, Ohio, 44128

Kraft Korner
5842 Mayfield Road
Mayland Annex
Cleveland, Ohio 44124

Leisurecraft
941 E. Second Street
Los Angeles, California 90012

Sax Arts and Crafts
207 N. Milwaukee Street
Milwaukee, Wisconsin 53202

Tepping Studio Supply Co.
3517 Riverside Drive
Dayton, Ohio 45405

Van Howe Ceramic Supply Co.
11975 East 40th Street
Denver, Colorado 80239

Western Ceramics Supply Co.
1601 Howard Street
San Francisco, California 94103

Etching Mordant

Allcraft Tool and Supply Co.
215 Park Avenue
Hicksville, New York 11801

Kilns

American Art Clay Co.
4717 W. 16th Street
Indianapolis, Indiana 46222

J. J. Cress Co., Inc.
1718 Floradale Avenue
South El Monte, California 91733

L & L Manufacturing Co.
144 Conchester Road
Twin Oaks, Pennsylvania 19104

Ludd Ucella
11482 Pipeline
Pomona, California 91766

Paragon Industries, Inc.
Box 10133
Dallas, Texas 75207

Skutt & Sons
2618 S.E. Steele Street
Portland, Oregon 97202

Precious Metals and Supplies

T. B. Hagstoz & Sons
709 Sansom Street
Philadelphia, Pennsylvania 19106

Pickling Compounds (Sparex)

Quimby & Co.
60 Oakdale Road
Chester, New Jersey 07930

Tools and Supplies

Allcraft Tool and Supply Co.
215 Park Avenue
Hicksville, New York 11801

Anchor Tool & Supply Co.
12 John Street
New York, New York 10038

C. R. Hill Co.
35 West Grand Avenue
Detroit, Michigan 48226

ENGLAND

Copper Shapes

H. W. Landon & Brothers, 9 Bartholomew Row, Birmingham 5.

Enamels

W. G. Ball Ltd., Anchor Road, Longton, Stoke-on-Trent, Staffordshire.

Blythe Colours, Ltd., Cresswell, Stoke-on-Trent, Staffordshire.

W. J. Hutton, Ltd., 285 Icknield Road, Birmingham 18.

Thomson & Joseph, Ltd., 46 Watling Street, Radlett, Hertfordshire.

Enamels and Kilns

Bernard W. E. Webber, Ltd., Webber Works, Alfred Street, Finton, Stoke-on-Trent, Staffordshire.

Wengers, Ltd., Etruria, Stoke-on-Trent, Staffordshire.

Gold and Silver Foil

Johnson Mathy Metals, Ltd., 73 Hatton Garden, London, EC1.

Geo. M. Whiley, Ltd., 54 Whitfield Street, London, W1.

Kilns

Kilns & Furnaces, Ltd., Kccle Street Works, Tunstall, Stoke-on-Trent, Staffordshire.

Sheet Copper

J. Smith & Sons (Clerkenwell), Ltd., 42 St. John Square, London EC1.

Special Tools

E. Gray & Son, Ltd., 12 Clerkenwell Road, London, EC1.

Index